PRAYER

Prayer

by
M. L. ANDREASEN

"The Book of Hebrews"
"The Faith of Jesus"
"A Faith to Live By"
"The Sanctuary Service"

PACIFIC PRESS PUBLISHING ASSOCIATION
MOUNTAIN VIEW, CALIFORNIA

Omaha, Nebraska   Calgary, Alberta

Library of Congress Catalogue Card No. 57-7779

Copyright, 1957, by Pacific Press Publishing Association

CONTENTS

INTRODUCTION

In some respects this is the most godless age the world has ever known. At the same time there is probably more praying being done than ever before. If this seems paradoxical, consider this:

Millions, even hundreds of millions of men have been called to arms in recent years. Most of the men who went into battle prayed, even if they had never prayed before. Many of the young men were away from home for the first time. They had been given a Bible or a New Testament, and were deeply moved as they bade farewell to loved ones and promised mother not to forget God. Millions of prayers ascended to God before each battle or invasion, as men lay in their foxholes awaiting the zero hour. Under such conditions men pray.

If millions of men who were called to the colors prayed, what shall we say of the millions of fathers and mothers, brothers and sisters, sweethearts and relatives who daily prayed for their loved ones in the service or on the battle line? It may be supposed that there was hardly a family anywhere that did not have some loved one for whom they prayed. And this is true not merely of so-called Christian countries, but of all. We are safe in saying that never has the whole world had its attention called to prayer as at this time, and never before have so many prayed. We read of men praying while hanging on to a plank with no help near; praying in a plane as it is shot to pieces and they are about to bail out; praying in dangerous outposts where death seemed certain—and God heard their prayers and miraculously saved them. From this we understand that while the evil one is at work maiming and killing, God is at work calling men to Him.

If we should inquire if this praying brought about a

corresponding permanent increase in godliness, we would regretfully answer that this does not seem to be the case. On the contrary, there has been a definite increase in juvenile delinquency, and an over-all increase in crime in general. It would be quite useless to cite statistics to confirm this; for the figures would be obsolete before they were published. Nor would a portrayal of actual conditions serve any purpose. The reader is fully aware of the definite decline in manners and morals. Conduct that was frowned upon a short time ago has become commonplace. There was a time when we thought conditions could never be worse; but we were mistaken.

How are we to account for these conditions in view of the much praying of which we have spoken? I believe that the reason can be found in the motives that activate the one who prays. Prayers and promises made because of fear or to escape danger are often forgotten when the crisis is past. As men looked to God from lonely outposts or foxholes, were their prayers grounded in a deep, abiding faith in God, or were they caused by mortal fear of death and of the possibility that shortly the men would have to give an account to their Maker? Did men who spent the last day of their leave in unnamable debaucheries and wild excesses of all kinds immediately change their course of action and turn to the Lord with their whole heart? As I visited army camps I was reminded of the times when mother sent me out to catch a chicken and get it ready for the oven. With a knife in hand I would chase the chicken, and pause for a breath as it evaded me. Instead of using the pause to get away from me as far as possible, the chicken ceased to run as soon as I did, and began to pick up scraps, apparently unaware of, and unconcerned about, the fate that awaited it. Some men exhibit no more sense than did my chicken.

Were there not many who found God in their war experience? Yes, many, thank God! But the overwhelming number forgot God and their promises to Him; and the result is seen in the upsurge of sin and crime in the war's after years, as is always the case. Nevertheless, God brought more men to a decision for religious faith in the foxholes than all the evangelists of earth could accomplish. His hand is not shortened; He has means of which men know little.

God at Work

God is not the author of war and calamity any more than He is of sin. But He uses these disasters to call men's attention to the only source of help. He has implanted deeply in every heart a consciousness of Himself to which men instinctively turn in moments of sorrow or danger. This can be explained on no other ground than that God has made the human heart for Himself, and that souls find no rest until they find it in God.

A national disaster comes, and men turn to God. High government officials are faced with a decision that may cost the lives of millions, and they appeal to heaven. A great responsibility is suddenly placed upon a man in high position, and we find a president on his knees. A family stands at the bedside of a loved one, and prayer is their only hope. Men who have never prayed before unashamedly acknowledge that their own resources are at an end. And so they pray.

Can we draw any other conclusion than that God has placed in the human heart longings and desires that ordinarily do not come to the surface, but become apparent in times of distress and danger?

> Deep in the human heart, crushed by the tempter
> Feelings lie buried that grace can restore.

God Is Willing

The fear or sorrow that awakens the consciousness of God may not be the highest motive for seeking God, any more than was the hunger that brought the prodigal son to turn home. But God is willing to accept almost any ground as long as it accomplishes His purpose. So the father received the prodigal with open arms, though the son's purpose was chiefly to get something to eat. God accepts and uses sorrow, hunger, affliction, disaster, fear, in calling men.

This conception of God's methods of work makes His presence very real to the believing soul. He sees God at work everywhere, using every means at His disposal to call men to repentance. He knows that God has not left Himself without a witness, and that every man has this witness in himself, "so that they are without excuse." Romans 1:20.

This should give the Christian worker a strong hope for success in his task of helping men to find God. He knows that God is at work and has implanted in every heart a responsive chord to the call of God. Men may resist the call; but with God on their side, they are not discouraged.

We therefore believe that the present is an opportune time to call attention to prayer and what it may do or not do for souls in need. The situation in the world demands a deeper consecration on the part of God's people. The work that must be done can never be accomplished by merely using better plans or new devices. It will not be finished by might or by power, but by the Spirit of God. It will be finished by prayer and deeper consecration, by men and women who know their God and who go forward in faith.

1

In God's Presence

IT IS considered a great honor and a rare privilege to be received in audience at a royal court, even though a hundred others are received at the same time. There is considerable rivalry among visitors to the British Isles to obtain the much-coveted invitation to a palace function where they are introduced to royalty. If invited, they spend much time preparing for the occasion. It is indeed the event of a lifetime. They read carefully the rules which govern their appearance, the proper way of addressing royalty, and what they may do or not do in the royal presence. The occasion is never forgotten; and if any remark is addressed to them by royalty, the words are ever cherished.

We need not attempt to compare or contrast such an occasion with that of appearing before the most high God in private audience. If the one is wonderful, the other is a thousand times more so. There can in reality be no comparison, only contrast; for God is beyond compare.

In prayer we enter the presence of God, the audience chamber of the Most High. Not, as on earth, are we ushered into an outer reception room with hundreds of others, but into the throne room itself, the inmost sanctuary of God, for a private audience with the ruler of the universe. It is doubtful that even the greatest of the saints fully appreciate the honor thus bestowed. And this honor is granted the lowliest of men! Wonder upon wonders!

In private prayer, as in public worship, we too often engage in communion with God as a matter of duty or custom and repeat certain phrases without thought as to their meaning. It is a pious practice learned from others or remembered from childhood. We cling to it as something we "ought" to do. We feel that if our prayers seem to do little good, at least they do no harm.

Such is a far cry from what God intends prayer to be. Prayer is not a common occasion for which no preparation is needed. It is an audience with God.

God's Plan for Man

We need to understand more about prayer than we do. Why does God want us to pray? He knows what we need, so why does He not simply give us what we ought to have? What are the conditions upon which rests the answer? What may we expect from prayer?

In God's universal plan men were intended to occupy a high position as co-workers with Him. To prepare them for this work they were to be subjected to certain tests to ascertain if they were worthy of their future high calling; if they stood these tests they were eventually to take their place as members of the household of God.

Such a plan involved a period of instruction and training which would demonstrate their capacity for learning the necessary lessons. During this time they would have the opportunity of deciding whether or not the life promised them by God as a reward for their work was worth the discipline necessary to meet the standard God has set for inclusion in His family. At any time they would be at liberty to terminate the agreement; and should they once more change their minds and wish to return to their allegiance to God, He would give them the opportunity, until they at last had irrevocably settled the question for or against God. If their decision was against life, they would eventually return to the earth whence they came. If they chose life and passed successfully their period of instruction and the final examination, they would be invested with life everlasting and be officially installed as the sons of God.

In the beginning there was open communication between man and his Maker. God was one with man, and the record states that He walked in the garden in the cool of the day. Prayer, such as we now know it, was unknown. Man did not fall to the ground when he talked with God. They communed one with the other as friends do and as Moses did later. "The Lord spake unto Moses face to face, as a man speaketh unto his friend." Exodus 33:11. There was perfect fellowship, as between father and son. God talked with man, and man talked with God.

After sin came in, this close fellowship ceased. Says God, "Your iniquities have separated between you and your God, and your sins have hid His face from you, that He will not hear." Isaiah 59:2.

While sin made a separation between man and God, and no direct communication was possible, man was not entirely shut off from God. A way of approach was opened through Christ, and in His name man could reach the ear of God. Jesus Christ declared, "No man cometh unto the Father, but by Me." John 14:6. "Whatsoever ye shall ask of the Father in My name, He may give it you." John 15:16. According to this, the way to the Father, and the only way, is through the Son. Through Him we may come, and whatever we ask in His name we shall receive.

This is the "new and living way, which He hath consecrated for us, through the veil, that is to say, His flesh." Hebrews 10:20.

This new way was first prefigured by the sacrifices offered to God in Old Testament times. These sacrifices were ordained to help man keep in mind that he was a sinner and as such deserved death, but that a way had been found by which he might come back to God and find access through the death of the sacrifice. Thus we find that Cain and Abel brought their sacrifices to God, "in process of time." Genesis 4:3, 4. In thus bringing a lamb from his flock, the sinner acknowledged his guilt and admitted that he was worthy of death. As he slew the animal he demonstrated that he understood that the wages of sin is death and that he was not worthy of life. The sacrifice also showed his belief that God accepted a substitute in his stead, and that the lamb died that he might live. Thus the sacrifice signified two things: man's acknowledgement of the justice of God in requiring punishment, and a demonstration of the mercy of God in providing and accepting a substitute to die in the sinner's place. On the sinner's part it was an act of faith for him to accept the provision and follow precisely the rules for the offering of the sacrifice.

The First Recorded Offering

In the first sacrificial scene mentioned in the Bible (Genesis 4:3-15), "Abel offered unto God a more excellent sacrifice than Cain, by which he obtained witness that he was righteous" (Hebrews 11:4). "Unto Cain and to his offering He [God] had not respect." Genesis 4:5. The difference between the offerings of Abel and Cain lay in the nature of their sacrifices. "Cain brought of the fruit of the ground an offering unto the Lord;" Abel likewise brought an offering of the fruit of the ground; but in addition "he also brought of the firstlings of his flock and of the fat thereof." Verses 3, 4. In bringing a lamb from his flock, Abel confessed that he had sinned and was worthy of death. He brought the lamb as a sin offering and asked God to forgive him and accept the lamb in his stead. Thus he showed his faith in the true Lamb of God. The Bible declares that "the Lord had respect unto Abel and to his offering: but unto Cain and to his offering He had not respect." Verses 4, 5.

In their simplest form, sacrifices were embodied prayers. It was at the altar that men met God, and here He accepted or rejected their prayers as they were symbolized by the offerings brought. Each offering had in itself the elements of prayer: confession of sin symbolized by the sacrifice; acceptance by God of the sacrifice, which meant God's acceptance of the sinner's prayer and repentance; and man's faith in both God's justice and His mercy. Sacrifices accepted meant sins forgiven. In each case where a sacrifice was brought and accepted, the record says, "It shall be forgiven him." Leviticus 4:26, 31, 35; 5:10, 13, 16, 18.

The offering of the sacrifices brought vividly to mind the seriousness of sin and the great cost of transgression; and the slaying of the victim by the sinner was intended to bring him to the decision, "Go, and sin no more." If this was the result of the offering, the aim of the sacrifice and the sacrificial system had been accomplished.

The True Meaning of Sacrifice

To the informed Israelite it must early have become clear that the sacrifice of an animal could not take away sin, but that it was only an object lesson to make more vivid to the mind that sin meant death, and that what counted was the sinner's attitude of repentance and confession. David understood this clearly when he said, "I acknowledge my transgressions: and my sin is ever before me." "Thou desirest not sacrifice; else would I give it: Thou delightest not in burnt offering." Psalm 51:3, 16. He then states God's real desire: "The sacrifices of God are a broken spirit: a broken and a contrite heart, O God, Thou wilt not despise." Verse 17. "The Lord is nigh unto them that are of a broken heart; and saveth such as be of a contrite spirit." Psalm 34:18. To this the prophets agreed. See Micah 6:6-8; Isaiah 1:10-20; Jeremiah 6:20; 7:21-23; Amos 5:21-24.

When Israel came to regard sacrifices in themselves as efficacious and forgot that what God demanded was a humble and contrite heart, God abolished the sacrifices. He still retained, however, the vital elements—prayer, a humbling of the heart before God, a broken spirit, a contrite heart, and an intense desire to go and sin no more. These are God's requirements today.

Not all believers in Old Testament times confined their prayers to the occasions when they brought their offerings. They prayed as we do now, and God heard their prayers. The prophets understood clearly that sacrifices were only a temporary arrangement, one that could safely be ignored when further light came. Hence we find prophets speaking lightly of sacrificial offerings while stressing spiritual attainments. Christ did not Himself bring any offering to the temple and He ignored all the temple ceremonies.

In Old Testament times it appears that prayer was more natural and unaffected than now. Men of old talked with God, and He answered them directly. Their prayers took the form of a conversation rather than of a formal petition. The prophets particularly appear to have been on speaking terms with God, generally getting their orders in dreams and visions, but also at times by word of mouth. While in some respects we may know more about religion than did the men of old, they knew far more about how to approach God. It is high time that we come back to communion with God and learn to "practice His presence."

"The Lord spake unto Moses face to face, as a man speaketh unto his friend." Exodus 33:11. From one such interview with God, Moses came down from the mount and was not aware that "the skin of his face shone" while he talked with God. Exodus 34:29. This reflection of the glory of God was so strong that Aaron and the people "were afraid to come nigh him." Verse 30. And so Moses "put a veil on his face. But when Moses went in before the Lord to speak with Him, he took the veil off, until he came out. And he came out, and spake unto the children of Israel that which he was commanded. And the children of Israel saw the face of Moses, that the skin of Moses' face shone: and Moses put the veil upon his face again, until he went in to speak with Him." Verses 33-35.

That God spoke with Moses face to face became so well known that even the Egyptians heard of it. Said Moses, "They have heard that Thou Lord art among this people, that Thou Lord art seen face to face, and that Thy cloud standeth over them, and that Thou goest before them, by daytime in a pillar of cloud, and in a pillar of fire by night." Numbers 14:14. It would be well if God's people at this time could come so close to God that men and nations would hear of it. The work would then be finished speedily.

2

Why Should Men Pray?

WHY should we pray? God knows all things. He knows what we need without our telling Him. A child does not beg his father for food, clothing, and shelter. These are provided for him as a matter of course. Why should we beg our Father in heaven for the things we need, which He knows we need? May we not take it for granted that God will give us what we need without having to be coaxed to do so? Why demean men by requiring them to beg on their knees for the things the Father should provide?

The answer is that God does provide for all, whether they pray or not, and He is no respecter of persons. He sends rain on the just and the unjust. Matthew 5:45. No one needs to beg for anything. God provides for all with strict impartiality. In fact, often the wicked prosper more than do the righteous. Doubtless for good reasons, God permits this. If He prospered only the righteous, and the wicked were cursed with poverty, some might turn to God for no other reason than the hope of reward. This would merely be a bribe to induce men to accept God, and such is inconsistent with God's plan or practice. God would have men make their choice for good or ill uninfluenced by hope of reward or fear of punishment in this life.

Because God treats all fairly and without bias, we find some men prospering financially while hating God. On the other hand, we find seemingly godly men barely eking out a living. The first work industriously, take good care of their herds and flocks, and are diligent in all that they undertake. The second are lax and careless, pray much and work little, and feel that God should support them. An unbelieving surgeon who has prepared well for his work may be more skillful and successful than the Christian physician who believes that he need not make such thorough preparation since God is on his side and will help him.

Why, then, pray? If God does not give special help to the one who asks; if he has to study as hard and prepare as much as the one who does not pray, why pray? If the praying farmer must work his field as thoroughly as does his nonpraying neighbor, of what advantage is prayer? Why should the medical student ask God for help when in the end he is not necessarily a better surgeon than his agnostic friend?

A Distorted View of Confession

These questions are all based on the assumption that prayer is a means of getting something out of God without having to work for it. The unbelieving man works for his success. Can a Christian substitute prayer for work? Not according to God's plan. Prayer definitely is not a substitute for work, or for anything else. Prayer and repentance may effect forgiveness; but ordinarily they will not change or even modify the consequences of evil done, nor will the penalty be remitted. David may confess and deeply repent of his sin, but the consequences are not removed. See 2 Samuel 12:13, 14. This is a principle that

men may forget and that needs to be called to their attention.

Some years ago one of my students had been dishonest
in an important examination. He was an average student,
but his examination paper was so good that he was given
a final B. Some time later his conscience disturbed him
and he wrote me a letter of confession, deeply regretting
that he had cheated. I answered him that I was glad he
had written. I accepted his apology and informed him
that I had changed his grade from a "B" to an "F." By
return mail I received an indignant protest against what
I had done, stating if this was the result of confession, he
would certainly never confess again. Did not his confession deserve a B? He failed to understand why I could
not report a B for work he had not done, and he failed to
see that the confession did not in any way alter the fact
that he had been dishonest and had not done the work
required for a B grade. Had a good grade been given
him as a result of his confession, it would be inconsistent
not to do the same for others who had also cheated, which
would clearly be unjust to all other students who had
honestly earned their grades. Confession that is based on
hope of reward is not true confession.

God does not bribe a man by promising him exemption from punishment if he will confess. True, there is
a reward for the obedient, but obedience or confession
based on reward is of doubtful value. In fact, it has no
moral value whatsoever. It is of the same nature as the
obedience of a child based on the promise of candy if he
will behave properly.

It was this principle that was at stake in the case of
Job. Satan sneeringly asked God, "Doth Job fear God for
nought?" Satan insinuated that Job's fear of God was
motivated by the fact that God had prospered him, that

he was religious because it paid him rich returns. God had put a hedge about him so that no evil could touch him; He had "blessed the work of his hands," and increased his substance in the land. Job 1:10. But if God should turn from him and cease to bless him with worldly goods, he would curse God to His face. Verse 11.

God accepted Satan's complaint, saying, "Behold, all that he hath is in thy power; only upon himself put not forth thine hand." Verse 12.

In initiating this trial, God was seeking to disprove Satan's contention that Job served God because it paid him to do so. He wanted to show that there was one man in the world who served God without selfish motives, one who would not renounce God though He removed His favors from him. In this matter God depended on Job, though Job was not aware of how much hung on his decision.

Armed with God's permission to deprive Job of his possessions, Satan took away from Job all he had, even his children. He did thorough work. The servants reported one calamity after another.

Stunned as was Job by these unlooked-for calamities, he calmly exclaimed, "Naked came I out of my mother's womb, and naked shall I return thither: the Lord gave, and the Lord hath taken away; blessed be the name of the Lord. In all this Job sinned not, nor charged God foolishly." Verses 21, 22.

Satan stood defeated. He had claimed that if God would take away from Job what he had, he would curse God. Instead of this, Job blessed the name of the Lord. It was a signal victory for God; for Satan himself had laid down the conditions of the test, and God had agreed to them. Job had not failed God. He had proved that at least one man did not serve God for profit.

Satan was defeated; but before long he came back claiming he had lost because God had not permitted him to touch Job bodily. If God would permit Satan to "touch his bone and his flesh," Job would curse God to His face. Job 2:5. God agreed to change the rules of the test, saying, "Behold, he is in thine hand; but save his life." Verse 6.

Satan now "smote Job with sore boils from the sole of his foot unto his crown." Verse 7. Job still did not know why God permitted this trial, but his faith did not fail. His wife advised him to curse God and die; but Job was not moved. "What?" he said, "shall we receive good at the hand of God, and shall we not receive evil?" The result was the same as in the first test. "In all this did not Job sin with his lips." Verse 10.

The test was ended. God had demonstrated that the accusations and claims of Satan were false. Job had not served God for reward. In triumphant words Job gives voice to his faith: "Though He slay me, yet will I trust in Him." Job 13:15.

Why Pray?

When the question is raised, Why pray? the background of the inquiry is that some supposed temporal advantage is to be gained by prayer, and that if there is no such advantage, there is no reason to pray. This puts praying on a commercial basis and ignores the true ground of prayer.

Prayer in essence is communion with God, conversing with Him as we would with a friend. Why do we associate and talk with our friends? Not to get something from them to enrich ourselves. The very thought of such considerations is foreign to true friendship or fellowship. Why do those who love each other like to associate one with the other, talk together, sit together? For the simple reason that they love each other. No other explanation is needed. Any supposed personal gain is far from their thoughts. Indeed, such a motive would be fatal to love. Love is based on giving, not receiving.

Why pray? Why love? We might as well ask, why breathe? One is as natural and necessary as the other. Where there is love, there is communion, there is prayer. It could not be otherwise.

Why pray? is a strange question to ask a Christian, for prayer is such a natural thing to him that he cannot conceive of life without it. If we should ask a little boy why he runs to his mother to tell her of his joys and sorrows, to show her some little treasure he has found, or tell her an experience he has had, he would be perplexed and wonder why such a question should be asked. Where else could he go? What else could he do? Mother can solve all problems. She is his source of wisdom. She can kiss away bruises; she can dry tears. She knows what to do in every case. Mother understands. At times he runs to her just to tell her that he loves her. The little pat on the cheek, the loving kiss, the sweet words, "Mamma loves you, too"—all these explain why he runs to mother. To him it is a strange and silly question to inquire why he runs to mother. He probably concludes that grownups don't know much. And he is right.

Likewise the Christian wonders how anyone can ask why he prays. He asks God for daily bread and receives it; but he knows that his unbelieving neighbor also gets bread without asking God for it. He knows that God feeds the ravens and the sparrows and wicked men. Then why pray? Because with the daily bread he receives something which the unbeliever does not receive because he does not ask for it, not being willing to comply with the conditions upon which the receiving depends.

As the child grows, the father knows that his boy will need more than food and clothing and daily bread. He will need companionship and fellowship. He will need the counsel of an understanding father. The son may not himself realize how much he needs such help; but the father knows and willingly does his best.

So with the father in heaven. He gives bread for the body to all; and to those who desire it He gives food for the soul and mind. He liberally offers this to all, but many accept the temporal food and reject the spiritual, to their own eternal loss. God offers it to them; He reaches out His hand to them, but only a few meet the hand of God. What more can God do? It grieves Him deeply when men reject His offer.

Why pray? Not primarily to get something out of God. Nothing is more worthy of condemnation than cultivating friendship for personal advantage. A sycophant is merely a vampire in human form. A friendship must not be used to extract gain.

Why pray? Because we are friends of God. There is nothing holier than friendship grounded in unselfish love. It is a bit of heaven on earth, a foretaste of the communion of saints in glory where the loves and sympathies which God has implanted in the human breast shall find fullest and freest expression.

Friendship

"Ye are My friends," says Christ. "Henceforth I call you not servants; for the servant knoweth not what his lord doeth: but I have called you friends." John 15:14, 15.

"Ye are My friends." Can anything be more glorious or wonderful? To have a friend whom you can trust, to whom you can speak freely, and to whom you can open the deepest recesses of the heart and know that he will understand; one who regards your confidence as a solemn trust not to be divulged; one to whom you can confide your most sacred longings and ambitions and who will not in his heart ridicule or belittle them; one in whose heart is locked your love and who reciprocates your feelings; one who will not mistrust you though he may not always understand; one who will defend you when others misunderstand and who will stand by you when the world turns against you; one who will refuse to suspect evil, though appearances are against you; one who, though absent or far away, remains the same; one who loves you though he knows your weaknesses, who will traverse the continent to be by your side in time of sorrow or of need; - one who will never leave you nor forsake you—this is the ultimate in human friendship!

If you have such a friend, hold on to him. Let not storm or tempest, rain, snow, fire, or water separate you from him; cling to him in life and death; commune with him; communicate with him; love him. We have such a friend in Christ. Never forsake Him. He will not forsake you.

Fellowship

Prayer is more than talking with God or talking to Him. It is fellowship with God, life with God. The highest joy in fellowship or friendship is not found in talking, but rather in the communion of spirits which transcends words. True friends may spend precious seasons together without speaking a word. Two may sit silently by the oceanside, hand in hand, and enjoy the sweet communion in silence. Two may walk together through the woods and enjoy communion with nature, with God, and with each other without a word spoken. Two may kneel in consecration, dedicating themselves to God and to each other, and there will be perfect understanding in the soul. There may be communion of heart and spirit without any outward recognition. Of words there may be none; but love, friendship, allegiance, are there, and quiet joy and surpassing happiness. Those who have had such experiences will understand the story of two lifelong friends who as life's shadows were lengthening would sit together of an afternoon without a word being spoken; and when evening came, one would express the feeling of both, "We have had a delightful time this afternoon." Those who understand this kind of friendship will never ask, "Why pray?"

Life with God may be experienced here and now. Heaven is not merely a future possession; it is a present reality. I am writing this while ten thousand feet in the air, flying over the island of Sumatra. The report from the captain has just announced the altitude, speed, temperature, and weather conditions. My dearest friends are far away; but I have never been more conscious of, or rejoiced more in, their love than at this moment. I know they love me; I know they are praying for me. In that love and knowledge I rest.

There is no more beautiful expression of the love of God than that found in Zephaniah 3:17. "The Lord thy God in the midst of thee is mighty; He will save; ... He will rest in His love, He will joy over thee with singing." The picture is that of a mother sitting quietly with her little one, singing in her joy and resting in her love, while the little one snuggles close to her breast. A most beautiful scene of rest, contentment, and love. This is the picture God uses in illustrating His love for us. He is ever thinking of us. As a mother quietly sings to her little one, so God sings in His love for us. He rests in His love. It is the height of peace and contentment for Him, whose nature is love. How can we help loving Him who first loved us? How can we help communing with Him when we get a glimpse of God and the fathomless love surrounding and enveloping Him? Prayer is communion; prayer is life; prayer is love; prayer is the breath of the soul. How can a Christian live and not pray?

Coming Home

When we get a clear view of the great Father heart of love, we can nevermore be disheartened or discouraged. God rejoices over us with singing, eagerly awaiting the time when all the children shall be home. Even now He is rejoicing in anticipation of that which is to come. He is happy in His love, and preparing for that great event of the ages, the homecoming of all the children of God in earth and heaven. Even to God this is a great day. While we are waiting for Christ to come, God is waiting for us to come. And His love and longing is even greater than ours. He has waited a long while.

And so we pray because we need God, need His love and fellowship, need His care and guidance. We pray because we love Him who first loved us, and because we find in Him a satisfaction of the soul not obtainable elsewhere. We pray not to get what *we* want, but to find out what *He* wants. We pray not to get Him to change His mind, but to have our minds changed. We pray not to have Him change His plans for us, but to ask Him to help us willingly to accept His plans. We pray not primarily to avoid pain, but for strength to bear it. We pray not to be taken out of the world, but to be kept faithful while in it. We pray not to escape hardship or trials, but for patience to endure them. We pray not to escape work, but for wisdom to know how to do it and do it well. We pray, first and last, because we love Him who has so loved us, because we treasure His fellowship and that of the saints.

It is a sad fact that with many Christians praying is a task that must be done, something that we *ought* to do, but for which we have no true urge, something which is a duty rather than a privilege. Such an attitude is not confined to lukewarm Christians. It is habitual with many persons who may be considered good Christians. In many cases this can be traced to a dim conception of the meaning of prayer and its possibilities. They *say* their prayers, they recite them; they have not learned to pour out their souls to God, and are getting only a few crumbs when they might have a full repast. Let such give study to prayer and its possibilities. Let them add to their prayers meditation. Let them learn to talk with God as with a friend, and they will find reaches of which they never dreamed.

3

Kinds of Prayer

THERE are several kinds of prayer, all addressed to God, yet each of a different nature. The most common kind is that of petition, wherein we ask God for some favor or a special blessing. We may pray for guidance, for protection, for success in an undertaking, for patience, for a deeper understanding of the things of God, or for any one of many other things. All such prayers are prayers of petition, and are acceptable to God. They are not often used alone, but are generally blended with other prayers, such as those of thanksgiving, praise, and adoration.

Prayers of Thanksgiving

Giving thanks to God for blessings received or for any other favors is most appropriate. Too often we accept blessings from God as a matter of course and forget to give thanks for them. Once Christ cleansed ten lepers and sent them to show themselves to the priests. Of these ten only one returned to give thanks to God. Said Jesus, "Were there not ten cleansed? but where are the nine? There are not found that returned to give glory to God, save this stranger. And He said unto him, Arise, go thy

way: thy faith hath made thee whole." Luke 17:17-19.
Paul exhorts us to give "thanks always for all things unto
God and the Father in the name of our Lord Jesus Christ."
Ephesians 5:20.

The pages of Scripture are embellished with prayers
of thanksgiving. The Psalms contain songs and prayers
of thanksgiving to the Lord:

> "O give thanks to the Lord, for He is good;
>   for His steadfast love endures forever!
> Let the redeemed of the Lord say so,
>   whom He has redeemed from trouble."

> "Let them thank the Lord for His steadfast love,
>   for His wonderful works to the sons of men!
> Let them extol Him in the congregation of the people,
>   and praise Him in the assembly of the elders."
>   Psalm 107:1, 2, 31, 32, R.S.V.

In our prayers we generally thank God for His many
blessings; but often the thanksgiving is a routine form
without any deep feeling. Saying grace at meals, thank-
ing God for daily food, is a commendable practice; but
that also may become a form without any real spirit of
thankfulness. In war concentration camps many learned
to give thanks to God for any little morsel of food, and
when liberated were perplexed that some seemed to take
food for granted and were not especially thankful for the
bounties set before them.

Prayer of Adoration

"Glory to God in the highest, and on earth peace, good
will toward men." Luke 2:14. This is a good example of
prayers of adoration. The angels were not asking for any
special favor; they were simply ascribing praise to God
for His wonderful gift to the children of men. When the

4

What Is Prayer?

PRAYER is not an exclusive Christian practice. All men pray, whether they be heathen, agnostics, idolaters, Buddhists, or of any other religion or superstition; men pray and have always prayed. History records prayers long before the time of Moses, and the Bible informs us that men shall pray to the end of time, even if it be only to the rocks and mountains.

Most of these ancient prayers were not, of course, prayers in the Biblical sense. They were generally offered only in times of emergencies, such as an earthquake, an important battle, a pestilence, prolonged drought, or some other great calamity. They were motivated by fear, often by desire for revenge on enemies; for the Christian concepts of love and concern for the welfare of others appear to be completely absent in some primitive peoples. Their prayers were prayers for themselves and for the destruction of their enemies. Utter selfishness lay at the root of such petitions.

From the beginning of time, men have found themselves face to face with forces of nature with which they could not cope. The thunders roared, the lightnings flashed, evil powers seemed intent on their destruction, and men stood helpless against the fury of the elements. A storm at sea would crush their stoutest boat, an earthquake would level their buildings, a volcano would spew out its molten lava, or a pestilence might decimate the people. Utterly helpless, men felt the need of pacifying the evil powers that were evidently intent on their destruction, and of imploring the help of the good gods who sent sunshine and rain and other blessings. Man has been called a praying animal, and not without reason. Prayer is part of man's nature, whatever his skin.

We call attention to this universal practice to stress the fact that prayer is a natural phenomenon common to all mankind. Many non-Christians pray habitually more than do Christians, as witness the Mohammedans and other Eastern religions. Prayer is inborn in man, a part of his nature. Missionaries capitalize on this implanted prayer habit and find it an excellent means of approach to uncivilized people. These people pray already. They need to have their prayers directed to the God of all, the One who made the heavens and the earth.

For the Christian, love of God is the true motive that leads him to pray. Fear, hatred of his enemies, selfishness, love of show, find no place in his thinking. He prays when he is in danger and asks God for protection from harm and accidents; he prays when he is sick or facing serious problems; but he has in mind that these are not the primary motives for prayer. The real ground lies deeper. And so we find that Daniel, when faced with the decree that under pain of death no one might pray to the God of heaven, "went into his house; and . . . kneeled upon his knees three times a day, and prayed, and gave thanks before his God, *as he did aforetime.*" Daniel 6:10. He did not change his practice because of the decree. This illustrates Christian prayer at its best.

An appeal to God for help in time of crisis is right and proper. The Bible is filled with examples of this kind of prayer. But we are to have in mind that this is not to be the prevalent form of prayer, nor is it of the highest kind. Prayer should not be dependent on a crisis. We are not to do as the little newsboy did. He said he never prayed to God except at night. In the daytime he could take care of himself.

Some are reluctant to call on God when they face a difficult situation, because they have neglected prayer previously. But God is always pleased to have us pray; so no one need feel hesitant. It sometimes takes a special event to start the prayer habit and supply the needed incentive; God recognizes this, and there are occasions when God Himself supplies the event. Israel "wandered in the wilderness in a solitary way; they found no city to dwell in. Hungry and thirsty, their soul fainted in them. Then they cried unto the Lord in their trouble, and He delivered them out of their distresses." Psalm 107:4-6. When some rebelled against the Lord, "He brought down their heart with labor; they fell down, and there was none to help. Then they cried unto the Lord in their trouble, and He saved them out of their distresses." Verses 12, 13.

"Fools because of their transgression, and because of their iniquities, are afflicted. Their soul abhorreth all manner of meat; and they draw near unto the gates of death. Then they cry unto the Lord in their trouble, and He saveth them out of their distresses." Verses 17-19. "They that go down to the sea in ships, that do business in great waters; these see the works of the Lord, and His wonders in the deep. For He commandeth, and raiseth the stormy wind, which lifteth up the waves thereof." "Then they cry unto the Lord in their trouble, and He bringeth them out of their distresses." Verses 23-25, 28.

These incidents reveal that the Lord uses all manner of means to call men to Him. He did that in olden times, and He does this today. And so we find a man on a raft in the midst of the ocean with certain death facing him, feeling after God and finding Him. An ocean liner goes down in a collision, and thousands pray while the band plays a church hymn. The president of a great nation wrestles with the problem of the emancipation of slaves, facing a decision that may cost much blood and even divide the nation; and finds his solution in prayer. A supreme council of world leaders gathers to decide questions that mean life or death to millions of innocent people, and every head is bowed in devout silence. God has many ways to incite men to prayer. The profound issues before the world teach men to pray as well as to think, and God uses them to further His aim.

God calls all men and uses all means. Men of erudition and scientific attainments, who never prayed before, are learning to seek God today. Working on weapons which threaten the annihilation of the human race, these leaders are appalled as they contemplate the use to which their inventions will be put. So God calls them, and some respond.

Men are discovering that human wisdom is insufficient for the world issues; that mankind is doomed unless some remedy is found. Humanity gropes for light. God is doing His part in awakening men's consciences as they realize the way the world is going. Scientists have released forces which they can no longer control, and men are making a desperate attempt to save themselves from themselves. In their dilemma they are turning to prayer in the hope that some higher power will come to their rescue. In doing this they are admitting their own failure and demonstrating that man cannot save himself—

a lesson that is being deeply impressed by current events.

At a time such as this it is well for the people of God to take stock of themselves. Have they any power in prayer that the world does not have? Are they taking advantage of the power which is at their command? Have they learned to pray? Have they learned to wrestle with God in prayer? And are they finding in prayer their stay and help? "Men ought always to pray." In a special sense this applies to our present time.

Prayer is the highest spiritual exercise of the soul. In its deeper form it passes into communion and fellowship with God, opens the door to the throne room of the universe, and converses with God as with a friend. In the earthly temple the Mosaic priest came nearest to God when morning and evening he offered incense on the altar. Likewise the Christian comes closest to God in his daily devotions, as his prayers ascend with the sweet incense of Christ's righteousness to the throne of the Almighty.

Some Christians consider prayer a duty to be discharged at stated times to please God. When they have performed their devotions, they rest content that they have done what is required of them. They feel that they have reminded God of what He might otherwise forget or neglect, but to which He will now doubtless give attention. God loves these dear souls who daily call upon Him as a matter of duty; and from heaven He sends the answer to their prayers when it is most needed. He knows the sincere desire of their hearts and overlooks their imperfect approach.

But most Christians pray not as a matter of duty but because they feel the need of communion with their Maker. Some use prayer books and recite the beautifully worded prayers prepared for their use. Others pray ex-

temporaneously, pouring out their soul's desire in their
heart's language which God understands. They pray for
loved ones, for missionaries in far-off fields, for the sick
and afflicted, for persecuted ones and those that suffer reproach for the Lord's sake; they humbly petition God for
forgiveness for their many shortcomings and for daily
strength, and then leave their case with God. God loves
to hear them pray.

More Than a Duty

The Bible not only encourages us to pray, but commands it. "Men ought always to pray," says the Saviour,
"and not to faint." Luke 18:1. This makes prayer a
Christian duty that should on no account be neglected.

But to the true Christian, prayer is more than a duty:
it is a high and blessed privilege. Paul speaks of love as
a duty when he says, "So ought men to love their wives."
Ephesians 5:28. There is indeed an "ought" phase to love
as there is to prayer. But in both cases the privilege phase
far exceeds the duty aspect. No man who truly loves his
wife considers it his duty to do so. To him it is not a
duty or a task; it is a privilege.

There are some vital questions that come to mind as
we consider prayer. Some doubt that prayer accomplishes
anything aside from the reflex influence it has on the one
who prays. Does prayer ever change the mind of God
and make Him alter His intent? Are answers to prayer
only wishful thinking? Is prayer effective in the field of
bodily infirmities? Is anyone ever healed of organic difficulty? Are souls saved because we pray? Is real communion with God possible? We shall consider these and
other questions as we proceed. It is time that we face the
subject of prayer realistically. This we shall do.

5

The Nature of Prayer

WE ARE persuaded that many expect from prayer that which God did not intend they should get. With their immature and even distorted view of prayer's purpose, they become discouraged when prayer fails to come up to their expectations. They crave great and immediate results, and when these are not promptly forthcoming, they are disappointed and tend to lose faith. For their sake, and for ours, we need a better understanding of what prayer can and cannot do.

The particular field in which prayer operates and to which it is limited is as definitely fixed as that of any other of the gifts of God. Grace has a vital place in God's plan, but it must work in harmony with law lest it trespass and enter a field not its own. Mercy operates under definite rules and conditions, as does forgiveness. Faith and works occupy a field where they have jurisdiction, and they must remain there, or conflict will result. Likewise prayer has its assigned sphere. While the full discussion of this is reserved for later chapters, we shall here make a few observations in regard to some of the common misconceptions of prayer.

Prayer is not primarily a short cut whereby Christians

may obtain freely that for which others must work. I need a certain sum of money and ask God for it. I doubt not that God *could* supply this money direct from heaven, nor do I doubt that God *would* do this if I really needed the money and there was no other way of getting it. God did a miracle for Christ once when He needed a coin to pay the temple tax. Matthew 17:24-27. But this is not God's ordinary way of working. The Lord gives "thee power to get wealth" (Deuteronomy 8:18); that is, He will supply the power, but we are to work for it.

It was on this same principle that God supplied manna from heaven for Israel. Said God, "I will rain bread from heaven for you; and the people shall go out and gather." Exodus 16:4. The Lord supplied the manna; but Israel had to gather it. This is how God works today. He supplies the rain and the sunshine, and causes the seed to grow; but man must plow, cultivate, and harvest.

If a request for money should come before God and we were able to hear the response, it would probably seem a disappointing one—at least to some. He might say, "Dear one, your prayer has been recorded, and I am sympathetic with you. I could send the money you need; but that would not be the best thing to do. I suggest that you follow the usual routine; work hard, and save. In the beginning I gave Adam work to do, because it was best for him. Genesis 3:19. I give you the same counsel. I will help you. I will stand by you. I will prosper you if you work hard and do not forget God's part of your earnings. But do not build your life on the proposition of receiving money from heaven."

Such an answer might seem cold and even cruel, especially to one who expects God to hand out money on demand. But God knows best; and there are few cases on record where God has answered otherwise. Let no

one misunderstand. God will send every angel in heaven
to the aid of one who is in need of help. Let him but call
on God, and the answer will come.

Prayer for the Removal of Pain

I have a severe pain, and I ask God to remove it. He
may do so if He thinks best, or He may let it remain, as
in the case of Paul who had "a thorn in the flesh" and
asked God to remove it. "For this thing I besought the
Lord thrice," he says, "that it might depart from me. And
He said unto me, My grace is sufficient for thee: for My
strength is made perfect in weakness." 2 Corinthians 12:
8, 9. God loved Paul, and Paul loved God. Yet God did
not remove the malady, but gave Paul grace and strength
to bear it.

When we ask God to remove pain, it is well that we
have Paul's case in mind. For reasons we do not know,
God may think it best to let the pain remain, and if so,
all we can do is to ask God for grace to bear it. We have
a right to pray, however. Paul prayed three times, as did
Christ in Gethsemane. But if, after searching our hearts
and dedicating all to God, asking that His will be done,
we receive no favorable answer, we may conclude that
God has some other plan for us, and we may pray as did
Paul, "Lord, what wilt Thou have me to do?" Acts 9:6.

God may know of reasons why it is not best for Him
to answer favorably a petition for relief from pain. That
reason may be hid from us; but it will be revealed to us if
we truly seek God and want to know His plan for us.
God may answer: "Dear one, I know you are suffering,
and I feel with you. I would gladly take away this pain
if this were the best thing to do. But before doing this,
I need your co-operation. If you should search your heart
you might find that there are reasons why you suffer. You

are not careful in your manner of living, in your eating and drinking, in work, rest, and recreation. You need to make some radical changes, and if you do, the pain will disappear. If you do all you can, I will help you. But it is necessary that you mend your ways. If you do not, and I should heal you, in a very short time you would again be where you are now. So, repent of your bodily sins as well as those of the heart. I will stand by you, and as we work together we will succeed."

This also may seem cruel comfort and cold advice, and some may think that God is not merciful. But good sense will confirm that prayer should not cover violations of the laws of health. Prayer is not to be used as a means to avoid the result of transgression. Someone has said, "Divine wisdom has given us prayer, not as a means of obtaining the good things of earth, but as a means whereby we learn to do without them; not as a means to escape evil, but as a means whereby we may become strong to meet it."

Prayer for a Conversion

If I should pray God to convert my unbelieving neighbor, He might well answer, "I will do what I can. But I must have your co-operation. What your neighbor needs is a demonstration of true religion in action. He does not believe that Christianity is of any special value. He sees little difference in the life of a believer and that of an unbeliever. If he could be convinced that Christianity really does something for a man, he would become interested. Do your best to convince him that Christianity has done something for you. Be kind, courteous, helpful. Do not irritate him with pious platitudes. Your life will preach better than your words. Be upright in all your dealings. Be fair, just, accommodating. Provide things honest in the sight of all men. Keep your house and your premises in order. Teach obedience to your children. If you will do this, I will be in a better position to help you answer your prayer. I need a man to whom I can point as an example of what Christianity is and what religion can do. Without such, I can do but little. Try this plan. I will help you. You are the man I want. As we work together, we may win your neighbor."

God is now looking for men such as Job, and He will find them in the last generation. When Satan sneeringly asks, "Where are those that keep the commandments of God and the faith of Jesus?" God will quietly answer, "Here they are." "Here are they that keep the commandments of God, and the faith of Jesus." Revelation 14:12. Satan will then get permission to test them, as he did Job; he will do his best to get them to fall. When at last he retires defeated and God stands justified, it will be because the saints have demonstrated that they serve God as a matter of principle and not for reward.

God uses every opportunity to enlist our help in the salvation of man. As a mother permits her little ones to help her, though they are more of a hindrance than a help, so God allows us to help Him. Whenever God can, He calls on us to assist, and gives us the credit.

An Ethiopian on his way home from Jerusalem was sitting in his chariot reading a portion of the book of Isaiah. He did not understand what he was reading, and he desired help. God could have sent an angel, but instead He commanded Philip to "go near, and join thyself to this chariot." Acts 8:29. Philip did so; he explained the scripture, and the man was baptized. Verses 37, 38. Philip evidently was anxious to go on other missionary endeavors, therefore the Spirit of the Lord took him away, and "Philip was found at Azotus." Verses 39, 40. Here was perfect co-operation between God and man.

God gave Nebuchadnezzar a dream, and He could as easily have given him the interpretation. But He called upon Daniel to give the interpretation. This made Daniel renowned in all the realm as a wise man, and as a result he became "ruler over the whole province of Babylon, and chief of the governors over all the wise men of Babylon." Daniel 2:48. God did the work; Daniel got the credit. Daniel understood this and gave God the glory. Nebuchadnezzar did not understand, took the glory to himself, and suffered the penalty. Daniel 2:27-30; 4:28-33.

These considerations and examples make it plain that God desires our co-operation, and that He is handicapped when He does not get it. He is anxious for us to become His colaborers, and as we do, He prospers and blesses. We may not expect favorable answers to our prayers unless we are willing to do our share of the work; but when we in faith and humility associate ourselves with Him, the reward is great.

Let us therefore repeat that God does not respond to our prayers unless we are willing to do our share. God has no intention of helping a lazy man or one who expects to get something from God without working for it. We are to work and pray as well as to watch and pray. Prayer, as well as faith, without works is dead.

Nature's Laws

These laws are not written laws, but rather denote events in nature which have been observed to occur with unvarying uniformity under the same conditions. In a certain sense these laws may be considered as God's laws, for the Creator who made nature also set forth the laws of nature under which all things, animate and inanimate, function. A water lily will flourish in a stagnant pool, where a rose will die. Fishes prosper in water, while land animals die if submerged. Plants will thrive in proper soil; in other soil they wither. These properties were implanted by the Creator in the beginning, and they still hold.

Even insensate objects appear to be under law. A timber of given dimensions will carry a certain load, and so will another timber of the same kind under like conditions. Increase the dimensions, and their load-carrying capacity will increase in a definite ratio. A steel cable has a certain tensile strength, and this strength varies with the dimensions of the cable, again with a definite ratio. Men have discovered what the ratio is, and have made up tables showing this. Every builder and structural engineer carries such a book of tables with him and depends on its accuracy. Without such uniformity confusion would result.

Even prayer must conform to law to be effective. Law, being the will of God, is supreme. All must bow to it. The earth beneath and the heavens above bear witness to the faithfulness of God. Let everyone who prays join God respecting law, and let him not ask God to violate any law in order to answer his prayer. Men may at times wish to have the law of gravitation temporarily suspended, or desire to have a moratorium on the law which says that as a man sows, so also shall he reap. Such prayers are in vain.

A Brighter Picture

This may seem a dark picture; for how can any man escape if he is amenable to law in which there is no pardon and which accepts no excuse? But there is a brighter picture. There is hope for the transgressor. "What the law could not do, in that it was weak through the flesh, God sending His own Son in the likeness of sinful flesh, and for sin, condemned sin in the flesh: that the righteousness of the law might be fulfilled in us, who walk not after the flesh, but after the Spirit." Romans 8:3, 4.

What the law could not do, God did. He provided a way of escape. He could not abrogate the law, but He could heal the wound that transgression had made. And this He did by sending His Son. By His wounds we are healed.

We have a faint picture of redemption and restoration in nature. In war, man may ruin a landscape and leave it in total devastation. But in a few years that same field presents a glorious view covered with poppies. An animal may be severely wounded, but it will lick its sores and start the healing process. A tree may be severely slashed by the ax, but it will do its best to cover the wound and is often remarkably successful. There are healing processes in nature which tend to repair any damage done. This is indicative of God's provision for man. The human race is not left to die alone because of transgression. Help is near. And God has means at hand to accomplish His design. He need not abolish any law in order to bring relief. Rather, He honors the law.

I never cease to marvel at the airplane. I see men load into the baggage compartment all kinds of luggage and heavy boxes. Then the passengers board the plane. I am convinced that the plane will never leave the ground; for have I not been taught that only a substance lighter than air can of itself rise from the ground? And the plane does not meet this specification.

But the plane rises. A miracle? No, only the application of other laws, laws of construction, of wing surface, of speed, which take precedence of the first law without abrogating it.

I know that a piece of iron will not float on water.

I make a demonstration to prove my point. The iron promptly disappears under the surface. I am correct. Iron will not float.

But a man comes along. "Change the shape of your piece of iron, and it will float," he says. I do so. I make of it a little vessel, a hollowed-out vessel, of the precise weight of my original piece that would not float; and, lo, it floats! A miracle? No, a simple application of the law of displacement. And then I wonder: If man by a change of the shape of an object can make iron float, may not God have a thousand ways of accomplishing His ends? God has, and He does not violate law to do so.

It is said of Columbus that at a banquet in his honor some persons made light of his discovery of America. Anybody could discover America. Just get in a boat and keep on going west, and there would be America!

Quietly Columbus handed an egg to one of his detractors and asked him if he could balance it on end. The man tried, but did not succeed. Handing the egg back to Columbus, he asked, "Can you do it?" Columbus took the egg, set it down hard on the table, cracking the shell, and the egg stood. "Well, it is easy enough to do it that way," said the detractor. "Yes," answered Columbus, "it is easy enough to do it if you know how." The onlookers saw the point.

"The Lord knoweth how to deliver the godly out of temptation." 2 Peter 2:9. Without doing violence to the meaning of the text, we may well use only the four first words, "The Lord knoweth how." What seems to us to be a miracle may not be a miracle from God's viewpoint. It may merely be an application of laws of which we are ignorant. In any event, the Lord knows how.

I stand appalled as I consider what God wants me to be, and the standard I must reach. I am convinced that there is no hope for me. But when I turn to God, I find One who knows how to deliver me, help me, and make me stand. I claim the promise, "He shall be holden up: for God is able to make him stand." Romans 14:4. I read: "Take unto you the whole armor of God, that ye may be able to withstand in the evil day, and having done all, to stand." Ephesians 6:13. I do not see how it can be done. But God knows how. As clay in the hands of the potter, so God can form us into a vessel of honor, if we will let Him. The motto, "Prayer changes things," may well be revised, "God changes things."

6

Prayer for the Beginner

THERE are doubtless those among the readers who have had little practice in prayer and who do not know the proper way to approach God. Some still remember their childhood prayers and use them; but these prayers do not always fit present conditions.

The first time I became seriously interested in religion, I with others faced the problem of prayer. I had heard a minister mention that Christ prayed all night, and though he did not suggest that others should do this, I drew the conclusion that all-night praying would be pleasing to God and deserving of a reward. I knew that I could not pray all night every night, but I might try it for one night. And so I attempted to do this.

My idea of prayer was to ask God for the things I wanted, and I thought that if I prayed long enough and earnestly enough, I would get my desire. God was a kind father, who sat in heaven and watched us, and if we boys behaved and were good we would get a reward. As I had been good for several weeks I was sure that God would hear me and grant my request.

So one night I started praying, intending to continue all night. There were not many things I wanted,—I thought I would be somewhat modest, at least to begin with,—and so my prayer was rather short, and I had soon said everything on my mind. What more was there to do? I could repeat what I had already said, but there seemed no special point to that. And how could I keep that up all night? I knew that ministers repeated in their sermons, but they used slightly different words each time, and I did not have those extra words. All I needed was a few minutes for my prayer, and I was done.

It did not take me long to conclude that it was not for me to pray all night. How could I find words to continue even one hour, much less all night? I decided that I needed a better education and a larger vocabulary if I were to pray for any length of time. I doubt that I spent as much as ten minutes in this first "night" of prayer. My prayer experience did not have a very promising beginning.

Wrong Conception of Prayer

The reader will immediately discern that I had a wrong conception of prayer. All-night prayer to me meant that I had to talk all night. Was not prayer talking to God, informing Him of conditions in general and of my own in particular? Was it not my duty to remind Him of what He should do, and make sure that He remembered what I had told Him before, but which He might have forgotten? Apparently God did forget things that I remembered. Had I not spoken to Him of many things and received no answer? I repeatedly asked Him to bless and protect my brother, and then my brother fell down and broke a leg! Surely God had forgotten what I asked Him to do.

I need not say that this was a disheartening experience and an unsatisfactory beginning for prayer. Every evening I would talk to God and get no response. Perhaps

God had not heard me at all. Perhaps I was too insignifi-
cant for God to notice. Perhaps I didn't count.

I thought God ought to hear me and make some kind
of response; but He didn't. What could I do to make God
take notice of me? I remembered how in school unruly
students received more attention than the good ones who
behaved. Perhaps I had been too good, and that was why
God let me alone. If I did something bad, God might see
it and do something.

I tried this in a small way, but God still ignored me.
What more could I do? As far as God was concerned,
I simply did not exist. I was too unimportant, too small
for God to bother with.

This state of things continued for some time. I finally
decided that if God ignored me, in retaliation I would
ignore Him. And I did. But that did not remedy matters.
I tried still to be some kind of Christian, but I felt that I
was not getting any help or encouragement from God.
He simply let me alone. And so I prayed only when I was
in dire need.

Then came the awakening—not in an abrupt way,
not by an angel coming down from heaven, or by an
arresting light at noonday, but simply by studying the
word of God, and by association with a man of God, one
of my own fellow believers. I had watched him as he was
preaching, and I felt instinctively that he had something
I did not have. But as I had been disappointed in God,
so I had also been in men; and I was certain that though
a man might make a good appearance in the pulpit, he
was "good" merely because I did not know him well
enough. If I should live with him, I would soon discover
that he was no better than others. All men I had known
before had feet of clay.

In the providence of God, as I now believe, I had the

opportunity of becoming well acquainted with him, of living with him. And, without going into detail, which would serve no purpose in this connection, I found him to be a true man of God, a man of prayer and of power. I saw prayers fulfilled before my eyes, undeniable cases of instant healing. This man lived in pain, and at times in outright agony, but with never a murmuring word. I tested him; I tried him; and he stood the test. Through him my faith in God was restored, faith in a prayer-hearing God. It was not his words that convinced me; it was his life.

While I shall ever be grateful for the help I thus received, it was not any man who taught me to pray. This was a gradual process as I began studying the Bible. Little by little, light dawned on me, and I began to understand the meaning and purpose of prayer. God ceased to be the kind of Santa Claus God I had conceived Him to be, and instead became a Father and a Friend with whom I could commune and counsel. I still needed to pray and thank God for daily bread, but I found that I needed counsel and spiritual guidance even more, and that God was abundantly willing to supply this also. It is hoped that the reader will experience the blessing and comfort that there is in real prayer, which in essence is fellowship and companionship with the Almighty.

Beginning to Pray

How, then, do we begin to pray? What do we say, what do we do? We know of no better or more simple, yet complete, prayer than that which Christ put in the mouth of the publican who stood alone and did not even dare to raise his face to heaven, but said, "God be merciful to me a sinner." Luke 18:13. The prayer was effective, for Christ tells us that "this man went down to his house justified."

Verse 14. We may therefore accept those seven words as the ideal prayer for one who seeks God, perhaps for the first time.

There are two couplets in this prayer that make it full and complete: God, merciful—me, sinner. The publican asked for mercy, knowing himself a sinner. He did not ask for justice: that would bring him face to face with the law, and "by the deeds of the law there shall no flesh be justified in His sight." Romans 3:20. The man did not parade his goodness or his wickedness; he simply asked for mercy. He made no excuse of any kind; he knew that God knew. And his plea for mercy, which came from an honest heart, was heard. No man who prays this publican prayer with a sincere desire to do God's will, need fear that he will be turned away. Like the publican he will go to his house justified. God hears such prayers.

Let the beginner who has never prayed before, or who has been disappointed in prayer, repeat from the heart these seven words: "God be merciful to me a sinner." Let him in all humility and faith come before God, and God will hear. The beginner must have faith to believe the promise: "If we confess our sins, He is faithful and just to forgive us our sins, and to cleanse us from all unrighteousness." 1 John 1:9.

"Without faith it is impossible to please Him: for he that cometh to God must believe that He is, and that He is a rewarder of them that diligently seek Him." Hebrews 11:6. There is one "must" in this quotation, or rather two, for "must" belongs equally to both statements; the first, "that He is;" and the second, "that He is a rewarder." Both of these statements are "musts." One who prays must believe that God exists—for what use would it be to pray to a nonexistent God? He must also believe that God is a rewarder of them that seek Him; that is, that God takes notice of those who pray, and rewards them according to their faith. God is not morally indifferent. He knows what goes on in the world, and rewards, or does not reward, as He sees best.

We suggest that the beginner in Christ ponder the prayer of the publican. As he utters this prayer he will search his heart and weigh his motives. He will come to the conclusion that there is hope for him only in the mercy of God, and he grasps by faith the promise that God will forgive if he confesses. And so he confesses. He does not use a set form of words. He pours out his heart to God as to a father, and as by faith he accepts the promise of the Lord that He will forgive and cleanse from all unrighteousness, he feels the burden roll off, and he claims the blessed promise to all who believe, that God will "abundantly pardon." Isaiah 55:7.

Let the reader who has not yet taken this first step hasten to do so. "Seek ye the Lord while He may be found, call ye upon Him while He is near: let the wicked forsake his way, and the unrighteous man his thoughts: and let him return unto the Lord, and He will have mercy upon him; and to our God, for He will abundantly pardon." Verses 6, 7.

This is the first step in coming to God, the first step in conversion. Let the inquiring soul take this step, and God will lead him on.

7

Does God Change?

DOES God change His purposes or His plans because men pray? Is anything at all changed because men desire to have them changed? These are serious questions, and they demand a serious answer.

It cannot be conceived that God, who from eternity has had a plan to which He is working, should change that plan or purpose because man wants it changed. "Like the stars in the vast circuit of their appointed path, God's purposes know no haste and no delay."—*The Desire of Ages,* page 32. "Above the distractions of the earth He sits enthroned; all things are open to His divine survey; and from His great and calm eternity He orders that which His providence sees best."—*The Ministry of Healing,* page 417.

In view of these statements some will immediately conclude that prayer does not and cannot accomplish anything. If God orders that which He sees is best; if His purposes know no haste or delay, man can no more change God's purposes than he can change the stars in their appointed path. Therefore, what use is prayer?

It is clear that God would not encourage us to pray and promise to answer, if nothing was accomplished by prayer.

The statement is clear: "The effectual fervent prayer of a righteous man availeth much." James 5:16. Just what does it avail?

In apostolic days prayer availed much. The lame were healed; the blind had their sight restored; the lepers were cleansed; the paralytics had the use of their limbs restored; even the dead were raised. Acts 3:1-8; Matthew 9:27-31; Luke 7:22, 12-15. In view of God's readiness to help us in answer to prayer, we are exhorted to seek the Lord while He may be found (Isaiah 55:6); to ask, seek, and know (Matthew 7:7; Luke 11:9); to watch and pray (Matthew 26:41); always to pray (Luke 18:1); to pray that we may be accounted worthy to escape (Luke 21:36); to pray with all prayer, and supplication, and thanksgiving (Ephesians 6:18; Philippians 4:6); to continue in prayer (Colossians 4:2); to pray for all men (1 Timothy 2:1); to pray everywhere (verse 8).

If we therefore are asked if prayer changes God, we would answer that prayer does not and is not intended to cause any change in God. His purpose is not changed. There are times when He may have alternate ways of working or may permit a certain choice of procedure, as in the case of David where He gave him a choice of three kinds of punishment because of his transgression: seven years of famine; three months of defeat in battle; three days of pestilence. 2 Samuel 24:12-14. God's purpose was not changed though David repented; but the king did have a choice of punishment.

Men Are Changed

If we were asked if prayer does not change anything we would definitely assert that prayer changes things, that prayer moves the arm of Omnipotence, that prayer can move mountains, clear away difficulties, heal the sick, change the entire course of a man's life, and even change history.

There are those who believe—and Christians among them—that prayer is primarily a means of getting something out of God, which He may hesitate to give, but which persistent prayer will effect. In support of this view they cite the account of the importunate widow who wearied the judge to the extent that he at last gave her what she desired, for no other reason than that she annoyed him. Luke 18:1-8. In like manner they believe that if they pray long enough, God will grant their request. They forget that the parable was given not to show what God is like, but what God is *not* like. God does not give men what they ask because they pray long.

Prayer is not primarily to get from God what a man wants, but rather to make man satisfied with what he has. It is not necessarily to relieve him from pain, but to give him grace to bear it; it is not to attempt to have God change His mind, but to have man accept God's mind. Prayer is not an endeavor to outline some plan of action for God to follow, but to ascertain what God's plan is and acquiesce in it; it is not to ask that God's will be *changed,* but that God's will be *done.* The chief aim of prayer is for the supplicant to come so completely into harmony with God that God's will becomes his.

If the real purpose of prayer is to bring a person into harmony with God, what has thereby been accomplished?

1. The man is now a partner with God and ready to co-operate with Him in whatever God wants done.

2. His mind has been taken from what he prayed for to something better. He has almost forgotten what he was so intent upon getting, and is now occupied with what God wants him to do.

3. He has learned what Paul did when he said, "I have

learned, in whatsoever state I am, therewith to be content." Philippians 4:11. Before, he fretted; now, he is content. He knows that he is in God's hand, that God is working out His plan with him, and that all things will work together for good.

4. He has learned to trust God fully, and has discovered that answer to prayer is not a problem to him any more. *All* his prayers are answered according to the promise, "What things soever ye desire, when ye pray, believe that ye receive them, and ye shall have them." Mark 11:24. A true Christian will ask of God only that which God wants him to have; his will is God's will, and he asks that God's will be done; hence, whatever he asks, he will get. He is in close touch with God, and sensitive to God's will.

Prayer is that simple. Learn to harmonize with God; attempt to ascertain His will. As soon as you have done this, your problem is solved. You may then ask for whatever you want, and expect to get it; for you will want and ask only for that which is in harmony with God's will, something He wants you to have. You will in all sincerity and simplicity inquire as did Paul, "Lord, what wilt Thou have me to do?" Acts 9:6. And God will make plain what He wants you to do. You will not continually be imploring God to do *your* will. You will leave the matter with God and be content. Christ was so sure that the believing suppliant would receive a favorable answer to his request that He could assure His disciples, "If ye have faith, and doubt not, ye shall not only do this which is done to the fig tree, but also if ye shall say unto this mountain, Be thou removed, and be thou cast into the sea; it shall be done. And all things, whatsoever ye shall ask in prayer, believing, ye shall receive." Matthew 21:21, 22.

Such answer to prayer can be true only where the one who prays is so completely in harmony with God that his will and God's are one. It was on this principle that Elijah worked when he suddenly appeared before Ahab and declared, "As the Lord God of Israel liveth, before whom I stand, there shall not be dew nor rain these years, but according to my word." 1 Kings 17:1.

Elijah's Attitude in Prayer

Elijah would never have dared use such language had he not had a previous understanding with God that He would support and confirm his word. God empowered Elijah to speak as he did, doubtless to enhance the prestige of His prophet, as would be the case when his prophecy came true.

As a result of lack of rain, a famine arose, and Ahab commanded that Elijah be found. When they met, Ahab accused Elijah of being the cause of the famine. Elijah answered that the real cause was Ahab himself in that he had forsaken God. He then took charge of the situation and commanded Ahab to gather all the prophets of Baal and Astarte together. Ahab would not have heeded Elijah's command had he not already been impressed with Elijah's authority. It is noteworthy that when God told Elijah to call Ahab, God said, "Go, show thyself unto Ahab; and I will send rain upon the earth." 1 Kings 18:1.

After the test on the mount had been completed, and it was time for the rain to come, Elijah prayed for it as if he were responsible for its coming. Seven times he prayed, and then the rain came. Verses 42-45.

This story of Elijah illustrates what Jesus meant when He said, "Ye shall not only do this which is done to the fig tree," but "greater works than these shall he do; because I go unto My Father." Matthew 21:21; John 14:12. To shut up heaven for three years was a greater miracle than causing a fig tree to wither and die.

We have no reason to believe that God at this time will cause mountains to be thrown into the sea at the command of a man. Nor do we in the least doubt that God could do this if the occasion called for it. Christ uses this extreme illustration to buttress His word that God will confirm what He has said, that "all things are possible to him that believeth." Mark 9:23.

Purpose of Prayer

In summing up what has been said in this chapter, we reach these conclusions: Prayer is not intended to procure for us the things we want from God. Prayer is primarily the way to bring us into harmony with God, so that His will and ours will be one. When this is brought about, peace and contentment will come to the soul. There is no longer any anxious pleading with God that He do our will, but a willing conformity on our part to accept whatever He sees is best for us. We will continue to pray as we have done before, but "our prayers will take the form of a conversation with God, as we would talk with a friend." And the conversation will not all be on our part; "He will speak His mysteries to us personally. Often there will come to us a sweet, joyful sense of the presence of Jesus. Often our hearts will burn within us as He draws nigh to commune with us as He did with Enoch." —*Christ's Object Lessons,* page 129.

In this sweet communion which may be ours, we do not keep asking for things any more than we would of an earthly friend. We are talking with God, telling Him our joys and sorrows, and getting from Him the counsel we need and the blessed assurance that He loves us.

8

Watch and Pray

WHILE we are admonished repeatedly in the Bible to pray, we are also counseled to watch. Matthew 24:42; 25:13; Mark 13:35. The reason given is: "Watch therefore: for ye know not what hour your Lord doth come."

To watch in the sense here used, is more than merely being awake. It means to be alert, to scan eagerly, to observe in order to look after, protect, or guard.

With many the word "watch" has lost its original meaning and has almost become synonymous with prayer. Hence the hour of prayer is often called "the watch hour," and the morning watch has become the same as the morning prayer. To this there is no objection, unless we fail to give watching an equal importance with prayer. There is danger lest, forgetting that watching and praying go together, we pray, but neglect to watch. Both have equal claims upon us.

In the texts mentioned above, "watch" has special reference to watching for the signs of the Lord's coming. This is most important, but the warning includes more than this. We are to watch lest we enter into temptation. Matthew 26:41. Satan has many ways of catching his prey, and we are to be fully awake and alert, or we may be caught in his snare. It is not enough to ask God to protect us and shield us from danger. We must take proper precautions ourselves. It should be known that faith in God is not inconsistent with doing all we can to help ourselves.

Young and old need to be on their guard. They should not ask God to do for them what He expects them to do for themselves. Lack of understanding of God's method of work has brought confusion and defeat to many. There are some things God expects us to do, and when we do our part, He will do His. God may send bread from heaven,—and will do so if needed,—but ordinarily we must work for it. God gives sunshine and rain, but we must sow the seed and do the harvesting.

Co-operation With God

Many Christians have been drilled in the belief that God does it all and that there is nothing for them to do but be pliant and submissive, and God will do the rest.

From one viewpoint this is true, but from another it is not. There are many things God cannot do without our help, and He asks for our full co-operation. Christ says, "As the branch cannot bear fruit of itself, except it abide in the vine; no more can ye, except ye abide in Me." John 15:4. But it is just as true that the vine cannot bear fruit without the branches. There is an interdependence between the branches and the vine that makes it necessary for both to work together. We cannot be separated from the source of spiritual power and live.

We say this in all reverence and only for the purpose of pointing out the necessity for our working together with God. For we well know that our part is only that of a willing medium who of himself can do nothing.

Such sayings as "Fear God and take your own part," "Fear God and keep your powder dry," "God helps those who help themselves," are at times used to belittle God. However, there is a certain amount of truth in them. God wants us to put our trust in Him, but not with our hands folded. If I am in financial straits, am I to call upon God for help, but do nothing to help myself? I seek God for health. Does this release me from being careful in my habits that I might glorify God in my body? I ask God to protect me from danger. Does that permit me to ignore a red traffic light? I am shipwrecked and about to sink. Shall I refuse the rope that is thrown to me? I pray God to protect me from accidents. I pray God to save me from temptation. Shall I then walk right into it, trusting God to save me? I fully believe that God can save me from my own folly if I transgress unknowingly; but I have no right to expect Him to perform a miracle when I insist on transgressing. God *can* save me if I ignorantly transgress; but if I deliberately drink poison I may expect to reap the consequences.

Watch and Pray

Therefore we are not only to pray, but to watch. We are to be on the alert for danger and take no unnecessary risk. While we are not to be suspicious of everyone and everything, we are to have our eyes open at all times. In the days of Nehemiah when the walls of Jerusalem were rebuilt and the enemies of God's people did all they could to hinder the work and there was constant danger of attack, the record reads: "They which builded on the wall, and they that bare burdens, with those that laded, everyone with one of his hands wrought in the work, and with the other hand held a weapon." Nehemiah 4:17. These men trusted in God, but they also watched. With all confidence they said, "Our God shall fight for us," but that did not hinder them from having weapons ready for an emergency.

God commands us to watch and pray, for the two go together. From the beginning it was God's plan to place His children in a position where they would be compelled to watch. That is why He placed the tree of knowledge of good and evil in the Garden of Eden. Had there been no tree there, Adam and Eve could have roamed the garden with never a thought of being careful where they went. The placing of the tree and the command not to eat of it, made it necessary for them to be on the watch. Had they watched and not gone near the tree, there would have been no temptation. Failure to watch caused the first sin.

It is well to shield children from temptation and from the sight of evil up to a certain age. But it is not well to make all decisions for them to the point where they are not compelled to make a decision and a choice for themselves. The time will come when as they grow up they will meet evil face to face. They should be prepared for such a time and not be left to meet temptation alone with no one to help. Under wise guidance, controlled experiments should be performed that would make them acquainted with certain situations and conditions and prepare them for the tests that of necessity will come. If they have not seen evil, if they have never been instructed to watch for its first innocent appearance, they may be taken unawares and caught in a snare that may have serious consequences.

Evil does not always appear repulsive at first sight. What could be more attractive than an artistically lighted room, beautiful music, and young, lithe bodies swaying in rhythmic motions as they dance upon the polished floor? To innocent eyes it does not appear wicked, and they reason that it certainly can do no harm. They do not know that there may be the beginning of a train of events that lead to blasted lives, unhappiness, divorce, insane asylums, homes for the incurables, and a pauper's grave.

The tree of knowledge of good and evil had every appearance of being a good tree. Eve could see nothing evil in it, and the fruit was inviting. But in the eating of that fruit was wrapped up murder in the next generation, and in seven generations the corruption of the whole earth.

I have seen children permitted to run wild until they feared neither God nor man. I have seen other children who were shielded from every temptation, but who, as soon as they were relieved from parental restraint, plunged into all manner of evil, largely because they were never permitted to face temptation under wise guidance. The parents of today need to be remembered in prayer; they need to pray themselves, for they are facing a task that is too great for human wisdom. Divine wisdom is needed to discern the line of distinction between unbridled liberty and wise restraint. Somewhere along the line, opportunity should be given young people for self-directed endeavor, for a natural introduction to the complexities of modern society, so that when they leave school or home they will be able to face life with some knowledge of the problems they will meet. They should not be asked to meet these conditions unprepared. Parents and educators should give careful study to their responsibilities, lest they send into the world young people who may have a good technical education, but who are totally unprepared for life.

The admonition to watch has many applications. We

are to watch our religious experience, for there is constant danger that we drift away from the old moorings. We are to watch the signs of the times, or we may find ourselves out of step with the opening providences of God. We are to watch our words, appearance, associations, recreations, habits, readings, Bible study, church attendance, financial dealings, and our account with God. There is no phase of life that we can safely omit.

As we watch we will discover dangers from within and without. Watching reveals these dangers to us, and prayer reveals the remedy. There are no circumstances under which we may not breathe a prayer; for prayer is an atmosphere rather than an appointed time and place.

Many things are going on in this world of which we are but dimly aware. In the air outside my window—and inside also—there are millions and millions of words and pictures flying around looking for a place to land and be transformed into audible words and visible images. They are as yet only electrical impulses, and how they ever become anything else I do not know. I see nothing as I look out; I hear nothing, but by turning a little knob on my instrument I can prove their existence. Suddenly the room is filled with music, and pictures appear. I see the President addressing a large gathering, and I hear him speak. I see the coronation taking place in England, and I hear the words of allegiance from those who kneel before the queen. I hear the explosion of a bomb thousands of miles away, and I hear and see the percussion. And I wonder, is there any good ground for not believing that the God who made all things may have a machine better than anything man has made that will record not only our words, but our thoughts, our intentions, and visibly reproduce every act of our lives? In view of what men can do, prayer becomes a reasonable possibility, and the advice to watch and pray is a sensible and reasonable request.

I am rolling along in my car on an excellent highway The weather is perfect, and there is no other car in sight. It is perfectly safe to exceed the speed limit,—no police are in sight,—and so I go sixty, seventy, eighty miles and all is well. But a mile farther on I am stopped and charged with speeding. Who saw me? Nobody followed me. But then I am confronted with a radar report! And there is the picture of the car and the speed noted electrically. Radar is no respector of persons. Its report is correct, and I am caught.

I need to be careful. I may think nobody is looking and I can safely transgress; but somebody *is* looking. God has a radar whose testimony I cannot gainsay. So I must watch, whether I see anybody watching me or not. I must watch for my own sake, watch for the sake of those who trust me. I must watch and pray.

I was discussing this in class once, and a student spoke up: "Well, if God has a radar, then I am sunk." The class period had not been in vain.

As God's watchmen, the ministry has a special responsibility. Says God: "I have set thee a watchman unto the house of Israel; therefore thou shalt hear the word at My mouth, and warn them from Me." "If the watchman see the sword come, and blow not the trumpet, and the people be not warned; if the sword come, and take any person from among them, he is taken away in his iniquity; but his blood will I require at the watchman's hand." Ezekiel 33:7, 6.

Personal Responsibility

The watchman's responsibility does not, however, relieve an individual from his personal responsibility. Christ, speaking to the disciples, said: "Watch ye therefore: for ye know not when the master of the house cometh, at even, or at midnight, or at the cockcrowing, or in the morning: lest coming suddenly he find you sleeping. And what I say unto you I say unto all, Watch." Mark 13:35-37.

While God thus holds the watchmen responsible, the Christian must also watch himself. Says Paul, "Examine yourselves, whether ye be in the faith; prove your own selves." 2 Corinthians 13:5. This means that each one must faithfully look into his own heart and attempt to discover whether he be in the faith. This entails more than examining certain doctrines to see if he is in harmony with them. It is more than adherence to a creed. It means first of all that a man must face himself with the question, Am I a Christian? Am I truly converted? Have I turned my back on the world? Am I a new creature in Christ Jesus? Am I an overcomer, or am I constantly being overcome? These are the questions that count. And high position or great learning do not come into the reckoning. We shall all appear before the judgment seat of Christ.

Such an honest self-examination will reveal weaknesses and faults that must be remedied. But no one need be discouraged though he finds himself far below the standard set by God, and even below the standard he has set for himself. Hear Paul's confession: "Not as though I had already attained, either were already perfect: but I follow after, if that I may apprehend that for which also I am apprehended of Christ Jesus. Brethren, I count not myself to have apprehended: but this one thing I do, forgetting those things which are behind, and reaching forth unto those things which are before, I press toward the mark for the prize of the high calling of God in Christ Jesus." Philippians 3:12-14.

Paul was a good man, consecrated and honest; but he confesses that he had not already attained, that he was not already perfect, that he had not yet apprehended. But this did not discourage him. He was determined to "follow after," to reach "forth unto those things which are before," and "press toward the mark for the prize."

Paul's experience should be an encouragement to all who with him have been pressing toward the mark, but who have found that they have come short and have not already attained or are already perfect. The un-Biblical "holiness" doctrine that is popularly preached may have done some good, but it has done much more harm. Were Paul now living, the believers in "holiness" would roundly rebuke him for recording his experience as in the quoted statements above.

Such an inventory as Paul made of himself, every Christian should make. He will discover his shortcomings and his sins, but he will not become discouraged. With Paul he will "follow after," and at last win the prize.

When we stated above that the chief problem of being true Christians cannot be determined by adhering to certain doctrines, some may have gotten the impression that we are not interested in doctrine, and that doctrine, after all, is not important. Let us hasten to remove such an impression.

Paul admonished his hearers not to do or teach anything contrary to the doctrine which they had learned. Romans 16:17. He had a definite "form of doctrine" which he delivered to them and which they obeyed. Romans 6:17. It appears from this wording that Paul had arranged a "form of doctrine" which he delivered to the church at Rome, and that they had accepted it and "obeyed from the heart." Some apparently had deviated from the "form" which Paul had given the churches, so he sent Timothy to stay at Ephesus and to "charge some that they teach no other doctrine." 1 Timothy 1:3. His counsel to Timothy was, "Take heed unto thyself, and unto the doctrine; continue in them: for in doing this thou shalt both save thyself, and them that hear thee." 1 Timothy 4:16. And in the last letter Paul wrote to Timothy before his death, he again referred to doctrine, saying to Timothy, "Thou hast fully known my doctrine." 2 Timothy 3:10. Having fully indoctrinated Timothy, Paul could safely leave him in charge, knowing that he would see to it "that they teach no other doctrine" than that which Paul taught. In this view of doctrine John joins Paul when he says, "Whosoever transgresseth, and abideth not in the doctrine of Christ, hath not God. He that abideth in the doctrine of Christ, he hath both the Father and the Son. If there come any unto you, and bring not this doctrine, receive him not into your house, neither bid him Godspeed." 2 John 9, 10.

In view of these statements, how can anyone think lightly of doctrine? When we are invited to examine ourselves whether we are in the faith, this faith may well include "the commandments of God, and the faith of Jesus." Revelation 14:12.

While there must always be liberty to differ on minor points, there must be unanimity on the great doctrines of the Bible held by the church.

9

Prayer and Meditation

PRAYER is to the spiritual man what breath is to the physical. No one can long survive without breathing; and no Christian will long continue as a Christian without prayer. There are individuals who are physically weak for no other reason than lack of life-giving air. If they would but open the windows and inhale God's free gift they might be well. But they continue to breathe stale, vitiated, and contaminated air and are slowly dying without knowing the cause. Renewed life might freely be theirs for the taking.

In the same manner some Christians are dying for lack of the life-giving breath of prayer. If they would but open their windows to heaven and draw deep breaths, their whole being would become invigorated, and new vitality and spiritual health would come to them.

Some persons neglect to pray because they have had an unsatisfactory experience with prayer. They have prayed, but God has not seemed to take any interest in them. With David they say, "My God, my God, why hast Thou forsaken me? why art Thou so far from helping me, and from the words of my roaring? O my God, I cry in the daytime, but Thou hearest not; and in the night season, and am not silent." Psalm 22:1, 2. They wonder if God has forsaken them and if it were better to cease praying. Their experience with prayer, their whole Christian experience, is unsatisfying. What are they to do?

Let such souls read and heed the following scripture: "My soul shall be satisfied as with marrow and fatness; and my mouth shall praise Thee with joyful lips: when I remember Thee upon my bed, and meditate on Thee in the night watches." Psalm 63:5, 6.

Note the glorious promise, "My soul shall be satisfied." This is exactly what these dear souls desire and what they are anxiously waiting for. They have prayed, and again and again they have hoped that God in some way would manifest Himself; but He seems to have forgotten them. So they pray again and again for years, but still no result. A few times they have had a taste of the joy that might be theirs, but it was only momentarily, and again they were left to grope their way. For them there is no balm in Gilead.

Now comes the joyful news that it is possible to find satisfaction in prayer. "My soul shall be satisfied." But how? Immediately follows the answer, "When I remember Thee upon my bed, and meditate on Thee in the night watches."

Meditation is the better part of prayer. In prayer we speak to God; in meditation God speaks to us. Not until we have learned the secret of waiting upon God will we enjoy the sweet communion that God reserves for those who wait upon Him. When we have learned it, the promise that we shall be satisfied will be fulfilled.

Note the reading carefully: "My soul shall be satisfied . . . when I remember Thee upon my bed, and meditate on Thee in the night watches." To this let us add two more statements: "My soul, wait thou in silence for God."

Psalm 62:5, A.R.V. "Stand in awe, and sin not: commune with your own heart upon your bed, and be still." Psalm 4:4.

Most Christians offer a little prayer at the bedside before retiring for the night. Having "said" their prayer they are ready for sleep. It is this little time between prayer and sleep to which the psalmist refers. He counsels us to remember God at this time, and meditate. Meditate is defined: "To think about; to contemplate; to plan, intend, purpose; to think deeply and continuously, to reflect, ponder, muse; solemn reflection on sacred matters." The psalmist calls this to "commune with your own heart upon your bed." Verse 4.

Man's Advantage

Man has this advantage over brute creation: He has the power of self-reflection and self-criticism. He can stand himself up in a corner, as it were, and examine himself. "Let a man examine himself." 1 Corinthians 11:28. "Examine yourselves; . . . prove your own selves." 2 Corinthians 13:5. This the Christian can do, and the unbeliever likewise.

The Christian can judge himself. He can do what God recommends, commune with his own heart upon his bed and think things through. Thus, when he has finished his evening prayer, instead of going to sleep immediately, let him spend a little time in self-examination and meditation.

"Amen" should not ordinarily be the end of our interview with God. When we do this, we are bidding God good night when He may not be ready to be dismissed. Saying "Amen" is "hanging up" on God, telling Him we are done, and cutting off communication. He may not think it courteous of us to talk as long as we please, and the moment we are done, cut off all further intercourse. We do not give Him opportunity to get in a word. Suddenly He finds Himself cut off. This cannot please God.

To avoid this embarrassment, God asks us to spend a little time in meditation. He wants us to be still and wait in silence. We might even pray as did Samuel, "Speak, Lord; for Thy servant heareth." 1 Samuel 3:9.

How do we commune with God? Have we not already prayed? Yes, we have prayed; and this is talking with God. But communion is more than talking. It is also listening. Of this we have done little.

The first step in communion is silence—silence in the soul, waiting upon God. "Wait thou in silence for God," we are told. You have prayed. Now you are lying upon your bed, ready to commune with your own heart. How is this done?

Consider this statement from *Christ's Object Lessons*, page 129:

"If we keep the Lord ever before us, allowing our hearts to go out in thanksgiving and praise to Him, we shall have a continual freshness in our religious life. Our prayers will take the form of a conversation with God, as we would talk with a friend. He will speak His mysteries to us personally. Often there will come to us a sweet, joyful sense of the presence of Jesus. Often our hearts will burn within us as He draws nigh to commune with us as He did with Enoch."

A Conversation With God

This is not an experience reserved for a few chosen ones; but is open to every Christian. Note again these soul-satisfying statements, "Often there will come to us a sweet, joyful sense of the presence of Jesus . . . as He draws nigh to *commune with us* as He did with Enoch."

God draws near to commune with us! What higher joy can earth hold? If God has such in store for us, should we not explore the possibilities of communion?

Someone will again ask, "Just what must I do to commune with God? How do I start? Be a little more specific."

It is not for one to tell another how to pray, but here is what one did.

"Lord, I have had a hard day today."

"Yes."

"I am tired, Lord, so tired."

"Yes, I know, dear one."

"I am afraid I lost my temper today, Lord. I was so nervous and tired out."

"Yes, I know all about it. I would gladly have helped you, had you asked Me."

"Lord, will You help me tomorrow? I will have another hard day."

"I will be happy to do so. But now you must go to sleep."

"Yes, Lord, I *am* tired. But before I go to sleep, I want to tell You that I love You. You have been so wonderfully good and patient."

"Yes, dear one, I love you, too. Now go to sleep."

"Good night, Lord."

"Good night."

Isn't this merely talking to yourself? says one. It is, but it may also be much more. Note again the promise quoted above, that on such occasions there may "come to us a sweet, joyful sense of the presence of Jesus . . . as He draws night to commune with us as He did with Enoch." If there is such a possibility, can we afford to pass it by?

God has good reasons for asking us to meditate and commune with Him in silence. As we pray we often talk aloud. Not only does God hear what we say, but we may also believe that Satan is an interested listener. He learns much of our plans from what we tell God, and uses this information to his advantage.

In meditation it is different. As we wait upon God in silence, Satan is completely at a loss to know what is going on. He cannot read our thoughts, and though he is expert at surmising, he can never be sure. What would not Satan give to learn what God is confiding to us?

Paul was once taken to the third heaven, and there he heard unspeakable words "which it is not lawful for a man to utter." 2 Corinthians 12:2-4. The original word for "lawful" is better translated "permitted" or "with permission." In Acts 2:29 Peter says, "Let me freely speak," literally "it being permitted me to freely speak."—*Englishman's Greek Concordance,* 7th ed., p. 268. It is the same expression as when we say, "With your permission I will speak freely." In Acts 8:37 Philip's answer in reply to the eunuch's question if he might be baptized was, "Thou mayest." In Acts 21:37 Paul asks, "May I speak unto thee?" In each case it is the same word that is translated "lawful" in 2 Corinthians 12:4.

Paul was taken to the third heaven, and there certain instruction was given him which he was to keep to himself and not tell anyone. God has secrets which He reveals only to those whom He can trust and who will not talk. This is in accordance with the principle enunciated in Amos 3:7, "Surely the Lord God will do nothing, but He revealeth His secret unto His servants the prophets." One of the first requirements of a prophet is that he will not talk without permission, that he will be able to keep a secret. God must have someone on earth to whom He can trust His secrets and who will be guided by them, but not reveal them to the enemy.

Does this mean that we are never to pray aloud? By no means. It is well that Satan listens when we affirm our faith in God and express our determination to go forward in faith whatever hindrance may come in the way. But there are some things we ought to talk over with God alone. This we can do in meditation.

If we should ask the reader if he has ever told God that he loves Him, he would doubtless answer, "Yes, many times. I have repeatedly testified to my love for God in social meetings and on other occasions." We doubt not that this is true. But it is not to this we have reference. Have you ever, as you are lying quietly upon your bed, looked up into the face of Jesus, as it were, and told Him, "I love You." *That* is real communion. And you may even have had blessed assurance of the words, "I love you, too." Such is the kind of fellowship for which God longs as much as we.

Boldness in Prayer

It is astonishing how formal we are with God. It is well that in public worship we approach God in reverence and godly fear. But are there not times when we as His children may come boldly to the throne of grace and there find help in time of need? Are there not times when we may speak freely with Him as with a friend, informally and confidentially? Is not this what John means when he says, "That which we have seen and heard declare we unto you, that ye also may have fellowship with us: and truly our fellowship is with the Father, and with His Son Jesus Christ." 1 John 1:3.

There is a boldness that is obnoxious and out of place, and which should be condemned and avoided. But there is also a boldness which is commendable and which God encourages. It is the boldness of a child who unafraid approaches his father, though he be a king before whom all men bow. To the child the father is not so much a king who is to be feared, as a father who is to be loved. The child does not speak to him as a servant does with fear and trembling, but as a child who has certain rights. Christians are invited to enter with boldness the holiest of all, the throne room of God, where only the high priest formerly entered (Hebrews 10:19); we are even to have boldness in the day of judgment (1 John 4:17). It seems almost unbelievable that such can be the case. And yet boldness is necessary for sonship according to Hebrews 3:6, where "confidence" is the word, otherwise translated "boldness."

As children of God we are to come confidently to God. We are to serve Him with "reverence and godly fear," and also "hold fast the confidence [boldness] and the rejoicing of the hope firm unto the end." Hebrews 3:6. As we do this we may at last be counted among those who not only are permitted to enter the pearly gates, but who "have *right* to the tree of life, and may enter in through the gates into the city." Revelation 22:14.

10

Prayer and Fasting

"THERE came to Him a certain man, kneeling down to Him, and saying, Lord, have mercy on my son: for he is lunatic, and sore vexed: for ofttimes he falleth into the fire, and oft into the water. And I brought him to Thy disciples, and they could not cure him." Matthew 17:14-16.

The disciples had been given power to cure diseases (Luke 9:1), but here was a case in which their prayers were ineffectual. Christ promptly "rebuked the devil" and cured the child. When the disciples saw this, they asked, "Why could not we cast him out? And Jesus said unto them, Because of your unbelief." Matthew 17:18-20. Then He added, "Howbeit this kind goeth not out but by prayer and fasting." Verse 21.

Christ had healed a disease which the disciples could not cure. Always before, when they had prayed, men were healed. But prayer did not avail in this case. This kind of disease did not go out but by prayer and fasting.

This brings us face to face with the problem of fasting. For a problem it is. If God will not hear when I pray, why should He hear when I fast? Will abstinence from food accomplish what prayer cannot do?

(71)

Many are perplexed about fasting. The church issues a call to fast, and the people fast, but are wondering what good it will do. All it seems to accomplish is to make them hungry, and perhaps irritable; they fail to see any good in that.

Some justify fasting on the ground that it is good for the body; that the mind also becomes clearer. This is doubtless the case with some; for the system might be clogged up, and fasting gives it an opportunity to dispose of accumulated surplus and give the organs a rest. But this cannot be the true reason for fasting. There must be other and weightier reasons.

"Jesus being full of the Holy Ghost returned from Jordan and was led by the Spirit into the wilderness." Luke 4:1. Matthew adds that He was led into the wilderness "to be tempted of the devil." Matthew 4:1. Mark gives the further information that He "was with the wild beasts." Mark 1:13. This tells us that it was God's appointment for Him to go into the wilderness, that the Spirit led Him there, and that He went for the specific purpose of being "tempted of the devil."

For thirty years Jesus had lived in Nazareth under ordinary human conditions. He had met the common temptations of childhood and youth, and now He was baptized and ready to enter upon His lifework. Thus far He had fulfilled all expectations. He had lived a blameless life, and at the baptism the Father had put His stamp of approval on Him. "Coming up out of the water, He saw the heavens opened, and the Spirit like a dove descending upon Him: and there came a voice from heaven, saying, Thou art My beloved Son, in whom I am well pleased." Mark 1:10, 11. It was immediately after this that the Spirit led Him into the wilderness.

As Adam was tested in the garden, so the second Adam

was also to be tested. But His test was to be a thousand times harder than Adam's. Adam stood in the full strength of manhood, and the test given him was the smallest conceivable. Christ's test came to Him after a grueling experience of a forty days' fast, when emaciated by lack of food He was near death's door, apparently forsaken of God and man, and His test was the hardest conceivable.

We have only a meager account of what took place during those forty days, for no human being was near to record it, and Christ has given us no information. We know that He was absorbed in His contemplation of the work before Him and the tremendous responsibilities that would be His. We know that He grew weaker day by day and that "He was afterward anhungered." We also know that "after the foe had departed, Jesus fell exhausted to the earth, with the pallor of death upon His face. . . . The angels now ministered to the Son of God as He lay like one dying."—*The Desire of Ages,* page 131. The Bible briefly states that after the tempter left Him, "behold, angels came and ministered unto Him." Matthew 4:11.

Christ went into the wilderness to contemplate His mission and His work. Before coming to the earth, in counsel with the Father, He had counted the cost and knew each step He must take. But now that He was man, He must once more consider His work from this new viewpoint, and as man decide upon His course. And this He did. As He found Himself "in fashion as a man, He humbled Himself, and became obedient unto death, even the death of the cross." Philippians 2:8. This decision He had already made in heaven; now He confirms it as man.

The question before Him now would be, could He, as man, carry out the covenant provisions made in heaven? Could He, as man, withstand the power of Satan and not

weaken under the assaults that would be made on Him?
The first thirty years were over. Now He is to appear
officially under the covenant agreement. Could He stand
the test? Hitherto there had been no special temptations,
but only such as are common to men. But now He had
come to a crisis. God had asked men to be faithful unto
death. Now Christ was to feel what this would be like.
Was He ready to resist "unto blood, striving against sin"?
See Hebrews 12:4.

He was overwhelmed as the magnitude of the task rose
before Him. Food was forgotten, rest was forgotten, the
wild beasts which surrounded Him—all was as nothing
compared to the test He must pass. As He daily grew
weaker, His determination grew stronger. He would be
faithful unto death. On Him depended the whole plan
of redemption; He must not fail.

And He did not fail. It nearly took His life, but having
made the decision, and having resisted the devil, He now
knew what He could do. He knew that He could stand
any test that would come to Him. In the wilderness He
had met Satan, and even in His weakened condition He
had won out. That experience and victory brought courage to Him in the days to come. He had met Satan on
his own ground and conquered him. He could do it again.

The True Fast

Christ's forty-day fast did not come about by a decision
on His part to go out in the wilderness and fast that many
days. It came about in a most natural way as He considered His lifework. He was so absorbed in His con-
templations and so overwhelmed with the cost of His
undertaking, that He gave Himself to prayer and meditation, and forgot everything else. In a minor way, men
experience similar reactions, wherein, because of the task

in which they are engaged, they forget everything else.

I have seen people in church promptly fall asleep as soon as the sermon is begun. I have known these same people to begin reading a book in the evening and become so interested in it that they would keep on reading all night with no thought of sleep.

There are those who become so interested in their work that they forget to eat and to sleep. Thomas Edison was one of these. He would become so wrapped up in an experiment that his food would remain uneaten on the table and his bed untouched, until he had solved the particular problem on which he was working. He was known to go without food and sleep for days. He was so interested in his work that creature comforts were neglected. Job felt this when he said, "I have esteemed the words of His mouth more than my necessary food." Job 23:12.

We may therefore confidently say, that true fasting comes as a result of absorption in the work we are doing. It is indicative of dedication in a high degree, of consecration to a task, of complete absorption in one's work so that we are oblivious of everything else. It was this that Christ experienced as they nailed Him to the tree. His agony of soul was so great that "His physical pain was hardly felt."—*The Desire of Ages,* page 753.

Moses when on Mount Sinai fasted forty days and forty nights, and "neither did eat bread nor drink water." Deuteronomy 9:9. After he had broken the tables of stone, he again fasted forty days. Says he, "I did neither eat bread, nor drink water, because of all your sins which ye sinned." Verse 18. Elijah also fasted forty days. 1 Kings 19:8. Such fasts were observed as a special preparation for a great work and closely connected with the presence of the Lord. When certain occasions arose and danger threatened, or some supreme event portended, men fasted. The spiritual part of man took precedence over the physical and dominated it completely, so that its needs were neglected. It is interesting to note that, when Moses took Aaron and the seventy elders with him to the mount, from a distance "they saw God, and did eat and drink." Exodus 24:11. Moses went farther up, and spake with God "face to face, as a man speaketh unto his friend," and he "did neither eat bread, nor drink water" for forty days. Exodus 23:11; Deuteronomy 9:18. Man can live forty days without food; but no man can live forty days without water unless a definite miracle is performed. That Moses did so signifies that God had complete control over him and that the spiritual controlled the physical. We are not told that Moses became weak or hungry because of his long fast. The physical nature was completely dominated by the spiritual. Fasting thus becomes symbolic of complete consecration.

Pharisees and Fasting

The Pharisees had made fasting a sign of piety and an opportunity for parading their religion. They put on "a sad countenance: for they disfigured their faces, that they may appear unto men to fast. Verily I say unto you, They have their reward. But thou, when thou fastest, anoint thine head, and wash thy face; that thou appear not unto men to fast, but unto thy Father which is in secret: and thy Father, which seeth in secret, shall reward thee openly." Matthew 6:16-18.

The Pharisees fasted twice a week (Luke 18:12), on Thursday, the day Moses ascended Mount Sinai, and Monday, the day he came down. When they fasted, they did not wash or bathe, or anoint the body, or shave the head, or wear sandals; but they put ashes on their heads.

Thus all men could readily see when they fasted, and give them due reverence. Of one of the Pharisees it is said that he fasted so often that his face was always dark —he never washed. In all this kind of fasting Christ showed no interest. It was not the kind of fast which He approved.

John's disciples fasted, but Christ's did not. The Pharisees noted this, and fastened on this as an excuse for arousing jealousy between the two groups. At one time, when Christ was eating with "many publicans and sinners," the Pharisees not only raised the question of the propriety of doing so, but asked, "Why do the disciples of John and of the Pharisees fast, but Thy disciples fast not?" Mark 2:15-18. Christ gave them a diplomatic and significant answer, and then dropped the question. He was not particularly interested in the matter. He did not condemn, nor did He favor. He left that for each to decide. But if they did fast, they were to do it so as not to be seen of men. Nevertheless, in the matter of the young lunatic, He let it be understood that some things cannot be done without fasting, and that for special occasions, prayer and fasting are necessary.

We are to conclude that in certain cases God will honor the prayers of His people only if they appear so much in earnest that they will deprive themselves of necessary food if need be that others may be helped. The disciples were evidently anxious that the young man be healed, but their predominant desire had not reached the point where they were willing to deprive themselves in order to help others. The story of the young man seems to teach that God will do something for a man who is deadly in earnest and who is willing to pay the cost, that He will not do for a man who is mildly interested in the case, but is not willing to deprive himself of anything or sacrifice to obtain the necessary results. A man who is willing to deprive himself of daily bread may be presumed to be in earnest. When a man gets to that point, God will hear, if by the healing God's name may be honored.

According to this, God leaves ordinary fasting to the individual conscience. But the servant of God who feels God's honor is at stake, who takes the situation so seriously that he is willing to do anything for his Lord and even deprive himself of needed food—God will honor that man and permit him to taste of "the powers of the world to come." Hebrews 6:5. In him will be a fulfillment of Christ's statement, that "the works that I do shall he do also; and greater works than these shall he do; because I go unto My Father." John 14:12. Fasting, as thus conceived, stands for complete and entire surrender, of wholehearted consecration, and sanctification. And thus fasting has a place even today. The great works that shall yet be done by the church of God will not be done without prayer and fasting. But let all beware of ostentation and any outward sign of mortification.

11

Why God Delays Answers to Prayer

THERE are many reasons why God does not answer all prayers, or why He delays to answer. The greatest reason is sin. Says the psalmist, "If I regard iniquity in my heart, the Lord will not hear me." Psalm 66:18. To "regard" here means to think well of, to be pleased with, to love. Of Christ it is written, "Thou hast loved righteousness, and hated iniquity; therefore God, even thy God, hath anointed Thee." Hebrews 1:9. Christ did not "regard" iniquity in His heart; He hated it. Therefore God anointed Him.

"Your iniquities have separated between you and your God, and your sins have hid His face from you, that He will not hear." Isaiah 59:2. Note these dreadful words: "Though they shall cry unto Me, I will not hearken." Jeremiah 11:11. "Yea, when ye make many prayers, I will not hear." Isaiah 1:15.

If the Lord does not hear our prayers, it is not because He is unwilling or unable to help. "The Lord's hand is not shortened, that it cannot save; neither His ear heavy, that it cannot hear." Isaiah 59:1. The Lord can hear what we say, but He may not answer, because sin has made a separation between Him and us.

This does not mean that we have to be sinless before the Lord will answer prayer. But it does mean that we must not regard sin, not love or harbor it, but hate it as Christ hated it.

This point needs to be stressed lest some become discouraged as they think of their sins of the past, and fear that God will not hear them. Does God not hear sinners? Most assuredly He does. If He did not, no prayer from human lips would ever reach Him; for "all have sinned." Romans 3:23. David himself sinned grievously; yet, upon repentance, he could say, "Verily God hath heard me; He hath attended to the voice of my prayer." Psalm 66:19. David had sinned deeply, but he repented as deeply as he sinned; and he no longer looked with an approving, covetous eye on sin as he had done before. Almost in surprise he exclaims, "Verily God *hath* heard me." If God heard David despite his sin, all may take courage. David committed adultery, and, worse, he murdered the faithful husband—a sin that would seem unforgivable. We repeat, if God heard David, we may be confident that God will hear us.

There are times when God does not answer our prayers immediately, and we are tempted to fear that He will not answer at all. This may be the case, but more often God waits until He in His wisdom decides that the time has come to respond.

There are three ways in which God may answer our prayers: He may say, "No;" He may say, "Yes;" or He may say, "Wait." The last answer is the most common, and in some respects the hardest; but it is always the most profitable for us if we have learned to wait on God.

One reason why God waits is to test our sincerity and earnestness. Do we really pray with an honest heart and a sincere desire to know and to do God's will and abide by the answer, whatever that may be? Or is our prayer but the whim of a moment? Are we like Pilate, who asked the momentous question, "What is truth?" and went away without waiting for an answer? John 18:38. His question was not grounded in a desire to know the truth in order to live it. It was merely an idle question asked out of curiosity. Speculative questions do not interest God. Pilate was not sufficiently interested to wait for an answer, so he never found out. "If any man will do His will, he shall know," says God. John 7:17. That is, only as a man will *do* God's will, will he in reality know. When we pray to God we should ask ourselves, Are we in dead earnest? Do we really want to know the truth for the purpose of doing it? Or are we playing with God and sacred things?

God Wants Us to Decide

Another reason why God does not answer all questions immediately is found in the fact that it is not best for us to have Him settle all questions. He wants us to wrestle with the problem ourselves and attempt to find the solution. This is based on the sound proposition that it is not good for anyone to have someone else do his thinking for him. God has given us our minds, and He wants us to use them. If He answered all our prayers, we would never need to do any studying or thinking. But God does not wish to deprive us of the opportunity of reaching our own conclusions, which is a vital factor in the formation of character.

Within limits, children should early be taught and permitted to make decisions for themselves. While this can easily be carried to extreme, as in ultramodern psychology, the practice in itself, if kept within proper bounds, is of definite value. When parents insist on making decisions for the children on every little point, they harm the child. Children should have increasingly greater responsibility placed upon them, should have opportunity to make decisions for themselves, so that when they are grown they can take their place in society fully competent to order their own lives.

At times parents are asked by their children to help them do their homework. The children find some problems which the teachers have assigned a little hard, and so they ask for help. It may be proper to help them, if it is done judiciously and in moderation. But if the parents habitually worked the problems for the children, they would do more harm than good. In the examinations held in school, such children would be sadly handicapped, having never had to work a problem unaided.

If God should solve all our problems, if He should answer all our prayers, He would make the same mistake that parents do when they work the problems for their children. God would ruin us effectively in so doing. As it is, God lets us use the strength we have, then He adds whatever we need, and we are the stronger for it. This is what Paul meant when he said, "Work out your own salvation with fear and trembling. For it is God which worketh in you both to will and to do of His good pleasure." Philippians 2:12, 13.

Problems in the Bible

For every difficulty we solve we will be stronger and more able to do more efficient work. If we are to build character into the life, we must learn to tackle difficult situations. To have every prayer answered promptly would be disastrous for us. God wants sturdy, self-reliant men and women. To develop that kind of people He gives them opportunity to work out their own problems as far as they are able. He will help; but He will give us only as much help as we need, not necessarily as much as we want.

There are problems in the Bible for which there are no ready solutions. This is in accordance with the principles here discussed. God wants us to study, to use the mind He has given us. He has made plain every great doctrine; all essential points of faith are clearly and authoritatively stated. There is no ambiguity, and hence there is no excuse for ignorance. But there are many questions God leaves for us to solve. He could easily have given us the solution as well as the problem, but He chooses not to do so. At times we wonder why God did not do things differently. To illustrate:

The Bible clearly states that we are to render unto Caesar the things that are Caesar's, and to God the things that are God's. All will agree that this is a sound principle. But the question readily arises: What things are Caesar's? What things are God's? On this there is no agreement among men, and God gives no definite answer. He leaves that for us to settle.

Tithing is a plain Bible requirement. But what is tithe? On this point opinions vary. Does it mean the gross income, or are certain exemptions permissible? And, if so, what? God leaves that question for us.

The question of Sabbathkeeping is another vital doctrine. On the seventh day we are to rest and not do our own work. What kind of work is permitted and counted essential? What is forbidden? Farmers have no easy task in determining how far they may go in doing essential work on God's holy day. Physicians are constantly confronted with problems relating to Sabbath observance. Who will settle them? Housewives, janitors, and ministers have their problems in Sabbath observance. In all these matters the individual conscience must decide. And God has a reason for this. The making of decisions is in itself character building.

The man who habitually decides every tithing question in his own favor is not building character for eternity. The same is true of those who decide questions of Sabbathkeeping too liberally, or any other question which God has left for man's decision.

Let us not be discouraged or perplexed when God does not answer promptly every question we bring to Him. He is waiting to see what we will do, and is giving us an opportunity to make our own decisions. The waiting time is a testing time, a time to search our hearts, to determine our motives, and to come to conclusions. In this work we may confidently ask God's help. He may not solve every problem for us,—we should not expect Him to,—but He can give hints and suggestions that will keep us on the right track.

God's delay in answering our prayers, therefore, is for a purpose. To solve every problem for us would be disastrous. God is too wise to do this. He gives us time to think things through. In our extremity He will step in, but we must use all our resources first.

12

Unanswered Prayers

WE ARE not to think that God has not heard our prayers because no favorable answer is given. The heavenly Father hears every prayer that is addressed to Him, but it is not always possible for Him to grant the request. For this there may be several reasons. We may not know what is best for us, and so may ask unwisely. God may have some better thing in store for us, and hence does not give us that for which we ask. We may ask for patience, and, knowing that tribulation works patience, God may send affliction as an answer to our request. Every prayer comes up before God and is given due consideration, and the answer sent is the one we would want if we knew all the circumstances as God does.

The Bible records many instances of answered prayers, and also many prayers that were not answered. When God denies a prayer, it is not necessarily because the petitioner is unworthy. Quite the contrary. We shall cite the cases of Moses and Christ in support of this view. It must be admitted that each of these men was dear to the heart of God, and that the denial of their prayers was not because God did not esteem them highly. Yet their prayers were not granted: Moses, because he failed to give God the glory; Christ, because He had taken man's place, and must experience the feeling of being forsaken of God as well as of man.

Moses' prayer that he be permitted to enter the Promised Land was a most natural one. Forty years he had herded sheep in the wilderness, and forty more years he had led Israel, until they were about to enter the Promised Land. He now stood before the entrance to Canaan and begged God pathetically if he might not enter. Hear him plead, "I besought the Lord at that time, saying, . . . I pray Thee, let me go over, and see the good land that is beyond Jordan, that goodly mountain, and Lebanon. But the Lord was wroth with me for your sakes, and would not hear me: and the Lord said unto me, Let it suffice thee; speak no more unto Me of this matter. . . . Thou shalt not go over this Jordan." Deuteronomy 3: 23-27.

This must have been a grievous, almost staggering disappointment to Moses. For this moment he had worked forty years, and now at the very time when he could have entered Canaan, God denied his request. He had been disobedient in what might be considered a minor matter. On a previous occasion God had asked him to *smite* the rock, while this time he was to *speak* to it. Instead of speaking as God had commanded, he smote the rock, and it gave forth water. Because of this disobedience God said to Moses and Aaron, "Because ye believed Me not, to sanctify Me in the eyes of the children of Israel, therefore ye shall not bring this congregation into the land which I have given them." Numbers 20:12.

In this case more was at stake than a rebuke to Moses personally. His punishment was a lesson to Israel as a whole. Naturally, Israel expected Moses to lead them into the land to the border of which he had brought them after these many years. Surely, God would not deny him the one thing for which he had toiled, prayed, and endured so many hardships!

When the news first reached Israel that Moses had been denied entrance, it must have caused consternation to the whole people. They had come to look upon Moses not only as their leader, but as their hope, their intercessor, God's chosen man. What terrible sin had he committed that he was to be set aside?

They knew that their fathers had died in the wilderness because of sin and lack of faith. But Moses! What had he done? It must have been some great sin beyond what the people could imagine, or God would not so deal with him.

It was therefore a matter of perplexity to them when they learned that Moses' sin was a seemingly trivial thing, one that did not deserve the punishment God had meted out. They knew that God was particular even in small things; but the fact that Moses had smitten the rock instead of speaking to it seemed so inconsequential that it would hardly deserve notice.

But God did notice it, and in such a way that it was not merely a rebuke to Moses, but a lesson to Israel in carefulness even in the smallest matters. The reason for Moses' ungranted prayer (Deuteronomy 3:23-27), was primarily his disobedience; but chiefly it was for the sake of the people who were largely responsible for his transgression and who needed to be shaken from their self-satisfied complacency. Said Moses pointedly, "The Lord was wroth with me for *your* sakes." Verse 26. They could not fail to understand that if God was strict with Moses, He would be no less strict with them. They needed to have this impressed upon them as they were about to enter the Promised Land.

Moses was not permitted to enter the Promised Land, the earthly Canaan. His request was not granted; but God had reserved some better thing for him. We do not know at what time Michael, the Archangel, "disputed about the body of Moses" (Jude 9); but we do know that Moses was taken to heaven, and that later he appeared to Christ on the mount of transfiguration (Matthew 17:3). Moses did not enter the earthly Canaan; he entered the heavenly instead. God's denial of his request brought Moses a greater reward than he asked for.

Jesus Christ

At the supreme moment in Christ's earth experience He prayed, "O My Father, if it be possible, let this cup pass from Me: nevertheless not as I will, but as Thou wilt." Matthew 26:39. The second time He prayed, "O My Father, if this cup may not pass away from Me, except I drink it, Thy will be done." Verse 42. After finding the disciples asleep, He "went away again, and prayed the third time, saying the same words." Verse 44.

We have no record of the answers which Christ received to His repeated prayers, except as they are suggested by the text. It appears that after His first request he was told that there was no other way by which the cup could be removed if He were to accomplish the task He had come to do. He had said to God, "All things are possible unto Thee" (Mark 14:36), which was true in itself; for God could have removed the cup; but that would have vitiated the plan according to which Christ was to give His life. It *was* possible for God to remove the cup, but it was not possible to do this and also save man.

This information must have been conveyed to Christ as an answer to His request, for He accepts the decision in the words, "If this cup may not pass away from Me, except I drink it, Thy will be done." Matthew 26:42. This prayer breathes complete submission after He understood that the cup could not be removed.

Christ's prayer to have the cup removed "if it be possible" can be understood only in the light of Christ's perfect humanity. He had taken man's place with man's limitations. Hitherto Christ had been one with God, and there had been perfect union and co-operation. But now He stood in a different relation to the Father. The sins of the world were placed upon Him, and He must bear the consequences. With the load of the world's sin resting upon Him, He must suffer the Father's displeasure because of sin. "Who His own self bare our sins in His own body on the tree," or as a more correct rendering has it, "up to the tree." 1 Peter 2:24. Being thus made sin for us, God must treat Him as we deserve to be treated, and must turn His face from His beloved Son.

Christ had fully understood the cost of saving man as He and the Father in the councils of eternity had evolved the only plan that could save man. He knew and understood Gethsemane, Golgotha, and Calvary. But now when He was man, clouds enveloped Him. He could no longer see His Father's reconciling face. All was oppressive gloom. It was one thing for Christ as *God* to decide to die for man. It was another thing for Him as *man* to pass through the dark waters alone. It was the realization of the necessity of being separated from the Father that broke the heart of the Son of God, and in His humanity He shrank from it. But faith broke through, and in submission He says, "Thy will be done."

Was Christ's request that the cup pass from Him denied? Yes, the cup was not and could not be removed. He must drink it.

Was His prayer heard? Yes. Hear these words: "In the days of His flesh, when He had offered up prayers and supplications with strong crying and tears unto Him that was able to save Him from death, and was heard in that He feared." Hebrews 5:7. Christ "was heard," but He was not saved from death nor from drinking the cup.

Are we then to draw the conclusion that God heard His prayer but denied the petition, and that the word "heard" here does not denote what it does in other places, namely, that of a favorable answer, but only that God heard what He said? Not necessarily; for in a larger sense God granted Christ's petition. This can be understood only as we appreciate the full force of the words, "Thy will be done."

In using these words, Christ submitted Himself so fully to the Father, that the Father's will became His. In this submission lay the answer to Christ's request. Christ's will was fully in harmony with the Father's; and as it was not possible to remove the cup, God's will became also Christ's will. Thus His prayer was answered.

With the examples of Moses and Christ before us, we should not be discouraged if our prayers are not answered immediately, or indeed, if they are never answered. There are good reasons for what God does. There are times when God ought not to answer our prayers for our own sake or that of others. In all conditions we are to submit to God, and whatever the answer to our prayers may be, we should from the heart be able to say, "Thy will be done."

13

Useless Prayers

THOSE who rejected the first message could not be benefited by the second; neither were they benefited by the midnight cry, which was to prepare them to enter with Jesus by faith into the most holy place of the heavenly sanctuary. And by rejecting the two former messages, they have so darkened their understanding that they can see no light in the third angel's message, which shows the way into the most holy place. I saw that as the Jews crucified Jesus, so the nominal churches had crucified these messages, and therefore they have no knowledge of the way into the most holy, and they cannot be benefited by the intercession of Jesus there. Like the Jews, who offered their useless sacrifices, they offer up their useless prayers to the apartment which Jesus has left."—*Early Writings,* pages 260, 261.

We are particularly interested in the last statement, "Like the Jews, who offered their useless sacrifices, they offer up their useless prayers to the apartment which Jesus has left." When Christ died on the cross, type met antitype, and the temple services ceased to be of value or have any spiritual significance. Yet the Jews continued to offer sacrifices, ignorant of the fact that Christ by His death had abolished them. It is to this custom of the Jews that the author has reference in the statement that the Jews offered useless sacrifices and that in like manner some now offer useless prayers to the apartment which Jesus has left. Just what is the meaning of this? Does anyone ever pray to an apartment?

To obtain an understanding of this, it is necessary to refer to the sanctuary built by Moses in the wilderness.

When God brought Israel out of Egypt to bring them into the Promised Land, He commanded them to build Him a sanctuary that He might dwell among them. Exodus 25:8. At this time they were wandering in the wilderness with no fixed abode, and they therefore erected a temporary structure, called the "tabernacle" or "sanctuary," which they could move from place to place. When Israel later entered Canaan, they erected a most magnificent structure which came to be known as "Solomon's temple," one of the wonders of the ancient world. While the temple was much larger than the sanctuary, both were of the same essential design.

The Building

The sanctuary was divided into two apartments: the first, called "the holy," and the second, called "the most holy." The first apartment contained three articles of furniture: the altar of incense, the table of shewbread, and the seven-branched candlestick.

The second apartment was called "the most holy" because this was God's dwelling place where He revealed Himself on special occasions. In it was the ark of the covenant, a wooden chest overlaid with gold, which contained the two tables of stone in which God had engraved with His own finger the Ten Commandments. The cover of the ark was called "the mercy seat," on top of which were the figures of two angels made of pure gold; and over the mercy seat hovered the Shekinah glory, emblematic of the presence of God.

There were no windows in the building, and the only light came from the golden candlestick, some of the seven lamps of which were always burning. The most holy apartment was dark, consonant with God's desire expressed to Solomon: "The Lord said that He would dwell in the thick darkness." 1 Kings 8:12.

None of the priests were ever permitted in the most holy place; the high priest only could enter one day in the year, while he performed his service there. As soon as he was done, the most holy was closed, and not opened again until the next year. The most holy was considered so sacred that no one might even be in the first apartment while the high priest was in the second.

The Service

The common priests served in the first apartment only, where each morning and evening they offered incense on the golden altar which stood close to the veil separating the two apartments. The meaning of the offering of incense is thus recorded by the revelator. He saw seven angels which stood before God. "And another angel came and stood at the altar, having a golden censer; and there was given unto him much incense, that he should offer it with the prayers of all saints upon the golden altar which was before the throne. And the smoke of the incense, which came with the prayers of the saints, ascended up before God out of the angel's hand." Revelation 8:3, 4.

As the priest offered incense, he also offered prayer, and his prayer with the incense came up before God as a sweet-smelling savor. On certain occasions the priest also brought with him blood from the sacrifices offered on the altar of burnt offering outside in the court, and a small part of this he put upon the horns of the altar of incense, while another part of the blood he sprinkled toward the veil behind which was the ark containing the law. The symbolism of this is clear: A man had sinned and had brought the required sacrifice and slain it. Then the priest had sprinkled of the blood on the altar of burnt offering. In case the anointed priest sinned, some of the blood was taken into the first apartment and there sprinkled toward the veil, in token of the law of God which the sinner had broken. This constituted a blood atonement, and as some of the blood was also placed on the horns of the altar of incense, the prayers that ascended to God with the incense also contained evidence of the man's repentance and of his belief in the atoning blood.

This service of incense and blood was carried on every day of the year in the first apartment, and as a result men obtained forgiveness. It is repeatedly stated that "it shall be forgiven them," "it shall be forgiven him." See Leviticus 4:20, 26, 31, 35; 5:10, 13, 16, 18. Hence the first apartment came to be known as the place where forgiveness was to be had.

On the Day of Atonement the high priest officiated in the second apartment. As stated above, while the high priest was in the most holy place no one else was permitted in the sanctuary, not even a priest. Should a sinner bring his lamb that day, he would find no priest to minister it for him. The attention of all was rivited on the high priest as he entered the sanctuary; and while he was inside, all Israel lay upon the ground seeking the Lord and praying that God would accept the ministration of the chief priest when he was in the most holy pleading for them.

Israel considered this day as a day of judgment, when

the sins of the year came in review before God. "Whatsoever soul it be that shall not be afflicted in that same day, he shall be cut off from among his people." Leviticus 23:29.

The Jewish Encyclopedia, page 286, article, "Atonement," quotes this concerning the Day of Atonement:

" 'God, seated on His throne to judge the world, at the same time Judge, Pleader, Expert, and Witness, openeth the Book of Records; it is read, every man's signature being found therein. The great trumpet is sounded; a still, small voice is heard; the angels shudder, saying, this is the day of judgment: for His very ministers are not pure before God. As a shepherd mustereth his flock, causing them to pass under his rod, so doth God cause every living soul to pass before Him to fix the limit of every creature's life and to foreordain its destiny. On New Year's Day the decree is written; on the Day of Atonement it is sealed who shall live and who are to die, etc. But penitence, prayer, and charity may avert the evil decree.' "

The Meaning for the Christian

These considerations are of absorbing interest to the Christian as he realizes that the temple services, including the services of the Day of Atonement, were symbolic of a higher service above in the heavenly temple, and that we have in Christ "such an High Priest, who is set on the right hand of the throne of the Majesty in the heavens; a minister of the sanctuary, and of the true tabernacle, which the Lord pitched, and not man." Hebrews 8:1, 2. As our Mediator, "Christ being come an High Priest of good things to come, by a greater and more perfect tabernacle, not made with hands, that is to say, not of this building, neither by the blood of goats and calves, but by His own blood He entered in once into the holy place, having obtained eternal redemption for us." Hebrews 9:11, 12. "For Christ is not entered into the holy places made with hands, which are the figures of the true; but into heaven itself, now to appear in the presence of God for us." Verse 24.

The work of the priests in the first, apartment of the sanctuary on earth, was confined solely to the forgiveness of sin. Forgiveness is good, but it does not go far enough. It was "a shadow of good things to come," but it was only a shadow "and not the very image of the things;" for never could the "sacrifices which they offered year by year continually make the comers thereunto perfect." Hebrews 10:1. All they did was to forgive sins *after* they had been committed. But forgiveness is not enough. Sin must be *stopped,* not merely forgiven. As long as men are satisfied with forgiveness; they will never reach the standard God has set. Christ came not merely to forgive sin, but "to *finish* the transgression, and to make *an end of sins,* and to make reconciliation for iniquity, and to bring in everlasting righteousness." Daniel 9:24. If a man has finished transgression, made an end of sin; when he has made for him reconciliation for iniquity and is in possession of everlasting righteousness, he stands approved of God. All this Christ came to do. Forgiveness of sin is wonderful; to have made an end of sin, is surpassingly wonderful. Such a man God can present as His finished product. Forgiveness is solely an act of God. Holiness is a product of God's and man's combined effort.

The High Priest

The high priest made a very thorough soul preparation before he dared present himself before God. He had to attain to a state of holiness in entering the most holy place; for without holiness no man shall see the Lord.

See Hebrews 12:14. Priests, as forgiven men, might enter the first apartment; but only a holy man could enter the second. That was why the high priest had upon his miter a plate of gold inscribed, "Holiness to the Lord." Exodus 28:36. This plate he must always bear. "It shall be always upon his forehead, that they may be accepted before the Lord." Verse 38. Even his garments had to be holy. Leviticus 16:4; Exodus 28:2.

This becomes of importance as we consider Paul's invitation "to enter into the holiest by the blood of Jesus." Hebrews 10:19. Only a holy man could enter then; only holy men can enter now. To go with Christ all the way, an expression we often hear, means to go with Him into the holiest of all; not merely into the first apartment, but into the second.

The time has come to take this advance step. Throughout the ages men have preached the glorious message of forgiveness of sin, and millions have turned to God and been converted. That message is still to be preached, for we will always need the forgiving power of God; and it is not possible to enter the second apartment without going through the first. But to God's elect He sends a message to come with Him by the new and living way which He has prepared for us. Those who thus enter with Him, He will keep from falling, while those who refuse to go farther, will sometime find their prayers to be useless. He who depends on God's promise of forgiveness and expects to sin and sin again, and keep on sinning and trusting to God's forgiveness, is presuming on the mercy of God. Let him believe that the Christ who came to make an end of sin, will also give him power to go and sin no more.

We are now ready to consider the statement quoted at the beginning of this chapter: "Like the Jews, who offered their useless sacrifices, they offer up their useless prayers to the apartment which Jesus has left."

A little girl who had done something wrong was asked if she ought not to ask Jesus to forgive her. To this she gave an emphatic No! The perplexed parents asked if she had not done wrong, which she readily admitted. But still she did not want to pray. Why? She said simply that she did not want to ask Jesus to forgive her. She hadn't quite finished what she was doing. She wanted to do a little more first and then ask forgiveness.

While we cannot recommend such a procedure, the philosophy in itself is not bad. She had the right idea that she ought to finish doing wrong before she asked forgiveness. It is useless to ask God to forgive us for stealing, if we intend to keep on being dishonest. We are to make an end of sin; we are to go and sin no more. It is useless to ask God to forgive us for breaking the commandments if we intend to continue in violation. God wants to do more for us than forgive our transgressions. He is waiting for us to claim the power that will keep us from sinning.

With God in Our Prayer Life

For us to enter with Jesus into the holiest of all, does not mean that we are to enter a room; it means that we are to enter into an experience comparable to that of the high priest who was getting ready to meet his God. To pray to Christ in the first apartment; to pray for forgiveness, and then sin and sin again, is displeasing to God. We are to enter with Him into the holiest of all and there find the help we need for holy living. Forgiveness in itself is wonderful; sanctification is still more so. God wants us to go with Him all the way.

In the parable of the Pharisee and the publican, one prayer was effective and the other useless. The Pharisee began by saying, "God, I thank Thee, that I am not as other men are." Luke 18:11. He was not an extortioner; he was not unjust, not an adulterer, not even as bad as this publican. He was a good man. He fasted and paid tithe. The publican's prayer was short, "God be merciful to me a sinner." He "went down to his house justified rather than the other." Verses 13, 14. The prayer of the Pharisee was unacceptable to God. It was grounded in pride and conscious superiority. Such prayers are in vain.

Once when Israel had sinned, "Joshua rent his clothes, and fell to the earth upon his face before the ark of the Lord until the eventide, he and the elders of Israel, and put dust upon their heads." Joshua 7:6. Joshua prayed earnestly and got an unexpected answer. "Get thee up," said God, "wherefore liest thou thus upon thy face? Israel hath sinned." Verses 10, 11. As Joshua hesitated, came the one word, "Up." Verse 13.

What was wrong? Was it not proper for Joshua to pray? God did not think so, not at that time. There was sin in the camp, and the first thing was to go vigorously to work and root out the sin. That was why God rather roughly told Joshua to get up and not lie there on his face praying and, when he didn't move fast enough, gave that one-word command, "Up," which doubtless made him move. God was teaching Joshua that prayer is not a substitute for action. Joshua was praying, but his prayer was not approved. There was work to be done.

Pharisees

Hypocrisy is one of the subtlest of sins. Christ might spare a poor sinful woman and refuse to condemn her, but when He found that the Pharisees "devour widows' houses, and for a pretense make long prayers," His wrath was aroused, and He did not spare. Mark 12:40. Their hypocrisy was their sin. He called them hypocrites, fools, blind, children of hell. Matthew 23:15, 17. "These shall receive greater damnation." Mark 12:40.

Why such language and such denunciations? It was not because of their sins as such, serious though they were, and meriting the rebuke. It was their hypocrisy that stirred Christ's soul. He declared to the Pharisees, "Ye also outwardly appear righteous unto men, but within ye are full of hypocrisy and iniquity." "Ye are like unto whited sepulchers, which indeed appear beautiful outward, but are within full of dead men's bones, and of all uncleanness." Matthew 23:28, 27.

Never before had Christ spoken so harshly. These men used religion as a cloak to hide their wickedness, and dared address the most high God in prayer. That was blasphemy, and Christ's whole being revolted against them. Their prayers were an insult to God.

Christ's reaction to the Pharisees measures His hatred of insincerity and pretense of any kind. Let all have in mind that the Pharisees were not the only ones guilty of this sin. Anything that savors of pretense, falsehood, lying, guile, fabrication, distortion, exaggeration, dissimulation, deceit, or misrepresentation is anathema with God. The Lord wants His people to tell the truth, live the truth, believe the truth, love the truth. In their mouth must be found no guile. Such people will do what they promise; they will be true to the truth though the heavens fall; they will be honest and fair; their word will be sacred to them, the conscience void of offense. And their prayers God will hear.

14

Forgiveness

WHEN we first come to God we may come just as we are with all our sins,—poor, and blind, and naked,—and God will receive and forgive us. He will not turn us away; He will not scold us; nor will He be angry. Our sins may be as scarlet, they may be red as crimson, but God, enfolding us in His arms, will cover us with His robe of righteousness and bring us in triumph to the feast which He has prepared. We are at peace with God, with man, and with ourselves. The former things have passed away, all things have become new, and with profound thankfulness we sing, "It is well, it is well, with my soul."

But after we are converted and are walking softly before God we suddenly become aware that the evil one has not left us alone, but has tripped us up, and we have made a misstep. We did not intend to sin, we did not transgress deliberately; but we are sorrowfully aware that we have come short of the glory of God. We have sinned. What are we to do? There is only one thing to do: Go to God and confess all, and if we have wronged others or hindered them in their Christian life, confess this to the ones concerned; and if restitution is indicated, attend to this also. If from a full heart we honestly do our part, God will forgive. He will abundantly pardon.

However, we should remember that there are conditions attached to this pardon, and that forgiveness is linked to these conditions. They are intended to help us remember to be careful in our daily walk and heed Christ's admonition, "Go, and sin no more." John 8:11.

These conditions are the same as those God prescribed for ancient Israel, and while Christians are not to observe the ceremonies which Israel had to follow, the principles are the same. It will stand us in good stead to review these ordinances, for they present to us in visual form what God wants us to do when we come short.

When an Israelite sinned, even though he did not know at the time that it was sin, "when he knoweth of it, then he shall be guilty." Leviticus 5:4. It was a merciful provision that he was not counted guilty until he was made aware that it was sin. But when he did discover that he had sinned, then he became guilty. He was not to pass the matter off lightly and excuse himself, because he did not know that it was sin. He had been guiltless before, but now he was guilty. This required confession. He was to "confess that he had sinned in that thing." Verse 5.

Confession Not Enough

It will be noted that God was not satisfied with a general confession. It must be specific and concern "that thing." Ordinarily it is easy to confess publicly that we come short in many things; but to make a specific confession is hard. To go to Brother Jones and confess that you have slandered and spoken evil of him, takes Christian courage. To go to a storekeeper and tell him that you have taken things out of the store and not paid for them, to ask his forgiveness and make restitution—this is real

Christianity and takes much grace. God demanded this of His people of old, and He has not changed.

To impress upon the sinner the sinfulness of sin, God required of Israel not only confession, but sacrifice. The sinner was to bring to the sanctuary an offering of a lamb or other prescribed animal for a sin offering, confess his sin, and then slay the lamb. After this the priest was to "take of the blood thereof with his finger, and put it upon the horns of the altar of burnt offering. . . . And the priest shall make an atonement for him, and it shall be forgiven him." Leviticus 4:28-31.

It will be noted that the sinner was to slay the lamb himself, doubtless to impress upon him the fact that he was guilty. It must have been a solemn moment when the priest handed him the sacrificial knife and commanded him to slay the lamb. As he plunged the knife into the innocent victim, he realized as never before the heinousness of sin and its great cost. He doubtless resolved never to sin again, which was the very effect God wanted to produce. He wanted to make vivid to the sinner that sin meant death and that the sinner should leave the temple grounds with the intention to go and sin no more.

This ritual of the lamb, the Christian, of course, does not observe. It pointed forward to the true Lamb of God, and after Christ came, the ritual ceased. The Christian has seen the true Lamb of God; he has seen the nails driven through the hands; he has seen the spear thrust in His side; he has heard the bitter cry, "My God, why hast Thou forsaken Me." He has seen the blood shed for him, and if these scenes have not produced in him the same determination as it did in the Israelite, to go and sin no more, then to that extent Christ has died in vain. Such a one may not have done despite to the grace of God, but he has most certainly grieved the Holy Spirit.

The ancient Israelite understood more of the plan of salvation than we sometimes think. He must certainly have received a lively sense of the sinfulness of sin; and he could not have failed to understand that the Lamb which he slew signified no less than the Lamb of God of which the prophets had spoken and which he had seen illustrated in the Passover lamb.

From this recital of how sins were forgiven in the old dispensation, we should have clearly in mind that forgiveness is not merely a matter of God's overlooking our faults, forgiving and forgetting them. Every sin required blood atonement; every transgression meant the death of an innocent victim. God can and does forgive, but the cost is Calvary.

We are always to confess our sins to God; but if the transgression is such that others are affected or involved, it may be necessary to make confession to man, and in certain cases to make restitution. If we have stolen ten cents or a thousand dollars, it is not enough to confess that we have done so; we must pay back that which we have stolen, with interest. As soon as Zacchaeus was converted, he said to the Lord, "Behold, Lord, the half of my goods I give to the poor; and if I have taken anything from any man by false accusation, I restore him fourfold." Luke 19:8. God does not require fourfold, but in some cases in the Old Testament one fifth was to be added. Leviticus 5:16. There is no rule in the New Testament in regard to adding a certain sum in addition to that which has been unlawfully taken; hence we take it for granted that this is left to the individual conscience.

There are some things that cannot be restored, especially where there have been slander, criticism, false witness. But though no real restitution can be made, they come under the general rule of confession and restitution.

Charity demands that every effort be made to undo the evil.

Where Others Are Involved

In cases of sexual misconduct care should be taken lest innocent persons be made to suffer because of confessions made. Where a case involves the husband or wife, and the sin is not known to the other mate or to the children, the procedure calls for great wisdom. While no hard-and-fast rule can be given, let all move cautiously lest harm be done by an unwise confession. In fact, it is only in very exceptional cases where confession should be made to an innocent person, though we can think of circumstances where it may be necessary. But often it may be best to let the matter rest and not bring sorrow and disaster to innocent parties. We do not feel free to give this advice in cases not personally known to us. It is too dangerous. We know of incalculable harm which has come from unwise advice.

In a certain church a deaconess had for years been a leader in good works and an example to the flock. Her reputation was unspotted, and she was held in high esteem. In her youth she had made a misstep, however, of which she had deeply repented. The man was not a church member, and the case was not known.

Twenty years had gone by, and then the partner in the transgression became converted and joined the church where the deaconess also was a member. He felt it his duty to confess his past sin, naming the deaconess as the other party. The pastor stood aghast. The deaconess's family was a happy one, and the two daughters were enrolled in one of our schools. What should the pastor do? He did not feel that the matter should be published, and yet he did not think the good sister should continue her work. So at the next election she was quietly relieved of her office.

This caused wonderment in the church. She was the one best fitted for the work. Why could she not serve? At last the news leaked out, and under the circumstances the sister felt it best to tell her husband. Result, a blasted home, a bewildered and crushed husband, a disgraced wife, and the two children called back from school where it had become impossible for them to remain. This was the result of one person's confessing for another.

Involving a Third Person

There may be times when it seems best to consult with some experienced and godly saint, one who will lock the confession in his heart and never divulge to anyone the secret entrusted to him. But let the confessor be sure that he selects the right kind of person. No woman should confess to a man alone, and no minister should permit a woman to confess to him alone. The pastor's study is not the place for confessions of that kind, since often he is in the building alone. What then, is to be done? If the pastor thinks it not best to have his wife present, let him select an old and trusted friend and let the two hear the case. Even then it may be best to stop the confession when it appears that no good will be gained by hearing it to the end.

One reason for discouraging confessions on this subject is that some people like altogether too well to confess. They seem to think that it gives them a certain standing. For once they are important and intend to make the best of it. They tell unnecessary details, and the pastor gets the uncomfortable feeling that they might not be averse to repeating their transgression. So let the young minister beware, and the old also. Hearing confessions of sexual misconduct is a dangerous practice. Let none be moved unduly by the penitential tear or the bid for sympathy. Danger is near. It is doubtful that hearing confession should be a large part of a minister's work. And this goes for the minister in a church and the revivalist in a school.

Let no one draw the conclusion that all confession should be discouraged or that counsel should not be sought. But let each penitent think twice before he bares his soul to a human being. It is in the confessional that the Catholic clergy get their power over their people. Let the minister beware lest he be contaminated by their example.

15

Prayer Expressions

THERE are certain expressions used in prayer the meaning of which is not always fully understood.

One of these is the common closing sentence of a prayer, "We ask this in the name of Jesus," or "Grant us this prayer, O Lord, because we ask it in the name of Jesus." These expressions are based on Christ's promise, "Whatsoever ye shall ask the Father in My name, He will give it you." John 16:23. The promise seems to imply that the name of Jesus will validate any claim.

This is a wonderful promise and opens the door wide to the believing soul. This promise, however, must be interpreted in harmony with other statements and not made to stand alone without any conditions attached. We may not, for example, ask God for permission to sin. We may not—as one man did—exact a promise from God to forgive him a certain sin he intended to commit. This man wanted to make sure that God *would* forgive it; hence he wanted God to bind Himself beforehand so he would be sure that it was safe to proceed. It is apparent that no magical words or a simple phrase will warrant God in giving us what we want. Our desire must conform to His will.

It will be conceded that whatever request we make of God should be within reason. We may not, for example, ask for the abolition of the Ten Commandments or the repeal of the law that the wages of sin is death. Such would be absurd. What, then, *is* the meaning of Christ's "whatsoever"?

When Christ made this promise, He was discussing the sorrows and disappointments that would come to the disciples at His death. While the world would rejoice, the disciples would weep and lament. Verse 20. However, soon their sorrow would turn into joy, which no man should take from them. Verse 22. At this point He makes the promise that whatsoever they ask in His name, the Father will give it to them. Hitherto they had asked nothing in His name. But now they would receive whatsoever they should ask, if only they asked in His name. Then He adds this significant statement: "These things have I spoken unto you in proverbs [margin, "parables"]." Verse 25.

From this expression it is evident that Christ gave them a blessed promise, but that it must not be taken in its extreme meaning, as it is a parable, a proverb. A proverb is defined as "a general truth stated in a graphic way." A parable is a simple story from which a lesson may be drawn. It must not be made "to go on all four," however; that is, it must not be interpreted too strictly or too extremely. The parable of the rich man and Lazarus is a case in point.

When Solomon says that "the liberal soul shall be made fat" (Proverbs 11:25), he states a proverb, a general truth: God will prosper those who are liberal. When he says that "there shall no evil happen to the just" (Proverbs 12:21), he states another truth, but it needs interpretation.

After Christ had given the disciples the promise men-

tioned above, He said, "The time cometh, when I shall
no more speak unto you in proverbs, but I shall show you
plainly of the Father." John 16:25. According to this
there is a difference between speaking in a proverb and
speaking plainly. We are therefore warranted in making
a difference also. In the present instance we need "to understand a proverb, and the interpretation." Proverbs
1:6. The interpretation seems to be this:

Understanding a Proverb

Christ was about to enter upon His mediatorial work.
Up to this time the disciples had never prayed to the Father in Christ's name. John 16:24. But Christ had now
finished the work He had been given to do. John 17:4.
He had earned the *right* of intercession. With boldness
He demands of the Father, "I will. . . ." Verse 24. These
were strange words for Christ to use. Before, He had
always said, "Thy will be done." But, having finished His
work, He had a right to say, "I will." In the covenant
agreement between Father and Son, Christ was to do His
part, and when He had done this, He had a right to demand that the Father do His.

"In the intercessory prayer of Jesus with His Father,
He claimed that He had fulfilled the conditions which
made it obligatory upon the Father to fulfill His part of
the contract made in heaven with regard to fallen man."
—*Redemption: or the Resurrection of Christ; and His
Ascension,* pages 77, 78.

"He had also a request to prefer concerning His chosen
ones upon earth. He wished to have the relation clearly
defined that His redeemed should hereafter sustain to
heaven, and to His Father. His church must be justified
and accepted before He could accept heavenly honor. He
declared it to be His will that where He was, there His

church should be; if He was to have glory, His people must share it with Him. . . . In the most explicit manner Christ pleaded for His church, identifying His interest with theirs, and advocating, with a love and constancy stronger than death, their rights and titles gained through Him."—*The Spirit of Prophecy,* vol. 3, pp. 202, 203.

In telling the disciples that henceforth they could ask the Father in His name, and God would do whatsoever they desired, Christ was announcing the new relation He sustained to the Father. He had *earned* the right of intercession. He had finished the work God had given Him to do; and it was now for the Father to do His part. "I will," says Christ confidently. Christ was yet to die. But thus far He had finished His work. John 17:4.

On the cross Christ finished another part of His work. "Jesus knowing that all things were now accomplished, . . . said, It is finished: and He bowed His head, and gave up the ghost." John 19:28-30. When Christ died—

"God bowed His head satisfied. Now justice and mercy could blend. Now He could be just and yet the justifier of all who should believe on Christ. He looked upon the victim expiring on the cross, and said, 'It is finished. The human race shall have another trial.' "—*The Youth's Instructor,* June 21, 1900.

In view of Christ's finished work He had a right to demand that all that had been promised to the One who should justify God in the eyes of the universe—and thus settle the controversy that had been initiated by Lucifer —be given Him. The Father freely granted this. With this knowledge and this assurance, Christ could confidently say to the disciples that henceforth they could ask the Father in His name, and they would receive. But this promise of the "whatsoever" must be held strictly within the provisions of the covenant agreement. It is not possible to introduce anything extraneous into the petition.

This is borne out by Christ's strange statement about what to expect from God in answer to prayer in Christ's name: "I say not unto you, that I will pray the Father for you: for the Father Himself loveth you, because ye have loved Me, and have believed that I came out from God." John 16:26, 27.

Interpreted this means: I can pray the Father for you, but it is not necessary that I do so, for the Father Himself loves you as He loves Me. And He loves you because you love Me. So all you need to do is to pray in My name.

Our first work, then, in praying, is to get Christ's endorsement. Before He will give this, our request must be in harmony with His general plans and desires. If we are to pray in His name, and if a name stands for what the person really is,—his character, the particular traits which make up the total personality,—then in taking Christ's name we identify ourselves with the characteristics of that name and become one with Him in ideals and purposes.

This changes the term "in His name" from a formula to a life. The question may therefore rightly be asked, Do we present our requests in His name, merely as a phrase added to our petition, or are we in character like the name?

A Blank Check

Some liken the promise that whatsoever we ask of God in Christ's name will be granted us, to a check on the bank of heaven, signed by Christ, but with no amount written in. That *we* insert. And the promise gives us authority to ask any amount we please. The check will not be dishonored, for it has Christ's name on it. We present it in His name. And God will stand by His promise.

This, they assert, is the meaning of the promise that we may ask anything in His name and it will be granted. But this would be unlike God's usual manner of procedure. Always there are conditions upon which God hears us. God never makes an unconditional promise. Christ never signs a check unless the amount is stated. That would be like the man mentioned above, who wanted God to promise to forgive a sin he intended to commit. The promise that God will grant any request whatsoever, if presented in the name of Christ, is interpreted by John to mean "that, if we ask anything *according to His will,* He heareth us." I John 5:14.

This, we understand, is the meaning of the promise. We must keep in close touch with God, ascertain what His will is, find out what He wants us to do, and then form our request "according to His will;" and He will hear us.

"Without the Loss of One"

There are some phrases often used in prayer that are well meant, but do not really express what we have in mind, and which should be revised or omitted. One of these is the pious wish, "Lord, save us all without the loss of one."

We call this a pious wish, for it is doubtless the sincere wish of the one who prays. But, generally speaking, it is a prayer that is impossible of fulfillment, for the simple reason that it is not possible for God to save anyone who will not be saved.

If God had His way, no one would be lost; for the Lord is "not willing that any should perish, but that all should come to repentance." 2 Peter 3:9. But the Lord does not have His way. He would gladly save all if He could; but having given man freedom of choice, He avoids the compulsion that would be a denial of the very freedom He has given. God will do the best that can be done under all circumstances; but let us not ask Him to do what He has left to the decision of someone else. We may ask God to help us do our part. But we must not think that when we have prayed we have done our part, and that it is for God to do the rest.

"No Visible Signs"

"We thank Thee, God, that there are no visible signs of Thy displeasure resting upon us." This is a dangerous prayer. For the fact that there are no signs of God's displeasure is no assurance that all is well. There were no visible signs in the days of Noah. Men ate, drank, married and were given in marriage, "until the day that Noah entered into the ark, and knew not until the Flood came, and took them all away." Matthew 24:38, 39.

There was no sign of God's displeasure in the days of Lot. "They did eat, they drank, they bought, they sold, they planted, they builded; but the same day that Lot went out of Sodom it rained fire and brimstone from heaven, and destroyed them all." Luke 17:28, 29. While we may be happy that there are no signs of God's displeasure resting upon us, this is not in itself conclusive evidence that God is with us.

"God Forbid"

"Forbid, O Lord, that I should have done anything this day displeasing to Thee." This also is a pious and well-meant prayer, but quite impossible of fulfillment. God Himself cannot forbid anything to be done that is done already.

God knows what we mean. We hope and pray that if we have done something we should not have done, that

He will forgive and blot out the record. This God can do, and this He will do if we ask Him. Such a prayer is an earnest wish to have the record clear. God is pleased with this kind of prayer.

We may all lean on the promise that if we do not know what to pray for as we ought, the Spirit will make intercession for us according to the will of God. Romans 8:26. So let us pray the best we know, but also rest in the confidence that if we fail to present our prayers as we ought, God knows the sincere desire of the heart, and will answer.

16

Bible Prayers

STUDY of the Old Testament shows that men then had as keen a sense of right and wrong as men do now. They knew what repentance and redemption meant, and most of them were aware that their sacrificial system was merely a temporary arrangement which would eventually be abrogated and that peace with God required more than bringing an offering to the sanctuary. A few examples will illustrate their grasp of religion and prayer.

The book of Job is generally recognized as the oldest book in the Bible, yet we find that Job had a clear perception of God and of His requirements.

Job was the richest man in all the East and was signally blessed of God. He had seven thousand sheep, three thousand camels, five hundred yoke of oxen, and a very great household. He also had seven sons and three daughters. Job 1.

The children did not follow in the footsteps of their father and, when they established their own households, spent their time feasting and drinking. There being ten of them, they took turns in entertaining, "and feasted in their houses, every one his day; and sent and called for their three sisters to eat and to drink with them." Verse 4. This caused great concern to their father, and each time when they had gone the rounds, Job sent and sanctified them and offered burnt offerings in their behalf; for Job said, "It may be that my sons have sinned, and cursed God in their hearts. Thus did Job continually." Verse 5.

The fact that Job sent for them and that they came, shows that he had not lost control of them entirely. Also, the fact that he surmised that they might have sinned and cursed God, shows that they had departed from the faith of their father. Job could not do much for them, but he did what he could.

Satan's Challenges

Following this opening account comes the story of Job's trials. When God called Job a good man and said, "There is none like him in the earth, a perfect and an upright man, one that feareth God, and escheweth evil," Satan responded to God's challenge. Verse 8. He sneeringly replied, "Doth Job fear God for nought?" Verse 9. He insisted that Job was just like other men and served God because it paid him to do so. God had blessed and prospered Job; so why should he not serve Him? If God should remove His blessings from him, Job would soon lose his religion. Said Satan, "Put forth Thine hand now, and touch all that he hath, and he will curse Thee to Thy face." Verse 11.

God accepted the proposal and Satan immediately began to deprive Job of all his possessions, including the children. But none of these things moved Job. He did not curse God as Satan said he would, but "fell down upon the ground, and worshiped, and said, Naked came I out of my mother's womb, and naked shall I return thither: the Lord gave, and the Lord hath taken away; blessed be the name of the Lord. In all this Job sinned not, nor charged God foolishly." Verses 20-22.

Job's second trial was harder than the first. To excuse his first failure, Satan claimed that God had not permitted him to touch Job, but only his possessions. If God would only let him touch Job's body, Satan said, "He will curse Thee to Thy face." Job 2:5. With the admonition, "Save his life," God permitted this proposal also, and Satan lost no time in attacking Job. But Satan again lost out. Patiently Job endured the torments of Satan, and when counseled to curse God and die, he replied, "What? shall we receive good at the hand of God, and shall we not receive evil? In all this did not Job sin with his lips." Verse 10.

Intending to comfort Job, three of his friends came to visit him. They were so astonished when they saw the calamity that had overtaken him that they judged it to be a punishment from God for some hidden wickedness. They counseled him to repent so that God would again bless him. This stirred up Job to defend himself. The friends made so many unjust charges that Job called them "miserable comforters." Where Satan had been defeated, Job's friends were about to succeed.

But then Job came to himself, and instead of bringing countercharges he began to pray for his friends. "And the Lord turned the captivity of Job, when he prayed for his friends: also the Lord gave Job twice as much as he had before." Job 42:10.

The book of Job begins with Job praying for his children. It ends with Job praying for his friends. And in prayer Job found victory. It is interesting that this oldest book in the Bible stresses prayer. And the prayers are not for Job himself, but for others.

It was no easy task God appointed Moses when He asked him to become the leader of Israel. The people were rebellious and continually murmured and complained, wishing that they had never left the fleshpots of Egypt. Somewhat bitterly Moses said, "Ye have been rebellious against the Lord from the day that I knew you." Deuteronomy 9:24.

But the rebellious attitude of the people did not deter Moses from praying continually for them. "Oh, this people have sinned a great sin," he said to God, "and have made them gods of gold. Yet now, if Thou wilt forgive their sin—; and if not, blot me I pray Thee, out of Thy book which Thou hast written." Exodus 32:31, 32.

To test Moses, God made him a wonderful proposition. "Let Me alone," said He, "that My wrath may wax hot against them, and that I may consume them: and I will make of thee a great nation." Verse 10. Instead of accepting God's offer, Moses began to reason with God, saying that the Egyptians would conclude that God had led Israel out in the wilderness "to slay them in the mountains, and to consume them from the face of the earth." He counseled God, "Turn from Thy fierce wrath, and repent of this evil against Thy people." Verse 12. "And the Lord repented of the evil which He thought to do unto His people." Verse 14.

One of God's Habits

In the beginning of the Bible we have the account of creation, and how "out of the ground the Lord God formed every beast of the field, and every fowl of the air; and brought them unto Adam to see what he would call them." Genesis 2:19. Note the reading: God brought the beasts and the fowls to Adam, *"to see what he would call them."* Each beast had its peculiar characteristics, and had been given a name corresponding to its character. As God had tested Adam's *obedience* at the tree of knowledge of good and evil, so now He tests his intellectual *knowledge,* his powers of discernment. God wanted "to see what he would call them." Could he discern character, was he observant? And Adam stood the test. "Whatsoever Adam called every living creature, that was the name thereof." Verse 19. Not, it *became* the name; it was the name already. Adam's judgment corresponded to God's, and thus Adam received credit for naming the animals. Verse 20. He could read character.

When God decided to destroy Sodom and Gomorrah because of their wickedness, He followed His usual practice of communicating His intent to His servants the prophets. Amos 3:7. So He talked the matter over with Abraham to get his reaction. Abraham evidently had misunderstood God's intent, for he thought God would destroy both the good and the wicked. Abraham did not think God should do this, so he rebuked God for intending to do such a thing. Said he, "That be far from Thee to do after this manner. . . . Shall not the Judge of all the earth do right?" Genesis 18:25. God, of course, had no such intention. But He wanted to get the reaction of Abraham; and He got it.

And so it was in the case of Moses. God tested him, but not for a moment did Moses consider God's proposition to make of him a great nation. He does not even refer to the matter.

Christ followed the same procedure as God. After His resurrection two men were on their way to Emmaus, and Jesus joined them, "But their eyes were holden that they should not know Him." Luke 24:16. They had the impression that Jesus was a stranger and proceeded to tell Him of the things that had happened, after He had asked, "What things?" Verses 19-24. Even when He answered them, He had so changed His voice that they did not recognize Him. When they came to the village, "He made as though He would have gone further." As they invited Him to come in, He evidently remonstrated with them, and only when they persisted and "constrained" Him, did He agree to stay. Verses 28, 29.

Why did Christ do this? To test them, as God had tested Adam, Abraham, Moses, and others. Christ wanted to visit with these two men, yet "He made as though He would have gone further." Did they really want Him to stay, or was it a courteous invitation that was not really meant? Christ tested them, and they demonstrated that the invitation came from the heart. Many times afterward the two recalled this incident and thought: What a loss it would have been had we not insisted on Christ's staying with us! This experience holds a deep lesson for the praying man today.

David

David was a man after God's heart. Naïvely he says of God, "Among the sons of my father He liked me." 1 Chronicles 28:4.

From all accounts David must have been a man of great physical charm, and also a wonderful character. For years he endured the unjust persecution of Saul, and when he had opportunity to kill him, refused to do so, "seeing he is the anointed of the Lord." 1 Samuel 24:6.

It was this man who was so sensitive that he felt condemned for having cut off Saul's skirt (1 Samuel 24:5), that had not the least compunction of conscience in killing a faithful husband whose wife he had violated! This made his sin so much greater. How could God ever forgive and forget?

Hear David's confession: "Have mercy upon me. . . . Blot out my transgressions. Wash me throughly from mine iniquity, and cleanse me from my sin. For I acknowledge my transgressions: and my sin is ever before me. . . . Hide Thy face from my sins, and blot out all mine iniquities. . . . Deliver me from bloodguiltiness."

Hear his prayers: "Create in me a clean heart; . . . renew a right spirit within me. Cast me not away; . . . take not Thy Holy Spirit from me. Restore unto me the joy of Thy salvation; and uphold me with Thy free Spirit."

Whatever view we take of David's sin, we are assured that he repented deeply. He knew that he had sinned, and he knew what are the wages of sin. He was willing to have God dispose of the case as He thought best.

If David was ever forgiven,—and he was,—his heart-felt repentance, as expressed in his prayers, availed much. David's confessions give evidence of his change of heart. That he recorded them, so that they have become a part of the Bible, shows that he did not intend to hide anything. What would one not give to have such a record forgotten? David was willing to have it published, as it would give hope to the vilest of sinners and show God to be the merciful God that He is. So what David suffered in reputation has been a source of help to many another poor soul. David did all he could to repair the loss.

From these examples of men who prayed, we may learn much. The men of old understood as much as we do of prayer, perhaps more. From all of them we may learn to be unselfish in prayer, to pray for others, to be persistent in prayer. May there not be times even now, when Christ will do as He did to the two men on the way to Emmaus, making "as though He would have gone further," when He is merely testing us to see if we really want Him to stay? It would be dreadful to have Christ go on His way, when He is anxious that we invite Him, and will come in if we only constrain Him.

17

Suffering and the Christian

DOES sickness serve any good purpose, or is it an evil, and only evil? When we are sick are we to ask God for healing, or are we to endure affliction and thank God for it? Does Satan cause sickness, or does God?

These questions have been discussed for ages, but no unanimous agreement has been reached. They are of sufficient importance, however, to warrant our giving attention to them.

Does sickness serve any good purpose? That depends entirely on the reaction of the sick one. In God's plan sickness serves a purpose, and an important one. It is one of God's instruments to help us develop an approved character.

God is not the author of sickness any more than He is of sin. He does "not afflict willingly nor grieve the children of men." Lamentations 3:33. Had sin not come into the world, there would have been no sickness. Nor will there be any in the world to come. In that good land "the inhabitant shall not say, I am sick." And the reason for this is stated in the next sentence, "The people that dwell therein shall be forgiven their iniquity." Isaiah 33:24.

God often uses sickness to accomplish His purpose, though it is only rarely that God takes an active part in inducing it. Ordinarily sickness is a result of sin, transgression of the laws of nature, and man is simply reaping that which he has sown. The word "ordinarily" should be noted. For while it is true that sin is generally the cause of sickness, it is not always the cause.

The Jews firmly believed that sickness was always caused by sin. Accordingly on a certain occasion, when the disciples found a man who was blind, they asked Jesus, "Master, who did sin, this man, or his parents, that he was born blind? Jesus answered, Neither hath this man sinned, nor his parents: but that the works of God should be made manifest in him." John 9:2, 3. We believe that there are similar cases today.

The Purpose of Sickness

Theologians hold that God is the *efficient* cause of sickness; that is, He is the source of all things and hence of illness. Sin is the *meritorious* cause; that is, sin merits sickness. Satan is the *instrumental* cause; that is, Satan is the one that brings it on. The enemy of man does this sometimes directly, as in the case of Job. At other times he uses transgressions of the laws of health, excesses, drunkenness, misuse of drugs, incontinence, and a thousand other things to lead men astray. In God's intent the purpose of sickness is to develop in the saints the sweet graces of patience and constancy in suffering, to enlarge their capacity for understanding and sympathy with those who endure affliction, and to mellow their spirit, getting them ready for the kingdom.

The man who is well and boasts that he has never been sick or had a real pain, does not know or appreciate what a migraine headache means to the sufferer and consequently fails to make allowance for him. He finds it hard to sympathize with a sick wife who has barely strength to drag herself around. He is well himself; why, then, should anyone else be sick? He is a "driver," and drives himself and all others. He is full of vitality, and if others are not, they ought to be.

For such a person sickness might be a definite help and blessing. When a man lies on the sickbed, he learns lessons not otherwise obtainable. Afterward he will be a little more understanding, a little kinder, a little more sympathetic. Up till now he has developed the more robust virtues of aggression, zeal, courage, and unflagging determination to push ahead. Now he needs lessons in the acquirement of some of the gentler virtues of patience, mercy, love, helpfulness, and understanding. And God knows how to bring this about.

I knew a surgeon once who had never known severe pain by personal experience, and who had little sympathy for those under his care who suffered, who dreaded pain. He was working on the wrist of a patient once and gave it a sudden twist which made the patient scream in pain. The surgeon looked at her in disgust: "Why, that doesn't hurt you!"

"No," answered the patient, "it doesn't hurt *you*." Had the surgeon not been especially competent, I doubt that he would have had many patients. He was too unsympathetic.

I discussed this with him one day; and while he admitted that perhaps he was rather unfeeling, he felt that most patients deserve little sympathy. They would complain before he had ever touched them; and if he catered to their fears, he would wear himself out completely. "A surgeon needs to steel himself, and not let a little pain disturb him." He was doubtless more right than I thought;

but, nevertheless, I expressed the hope that he would some time have a little taste of his own medicine. I told him that it would do him a great deal of good to be sick, really sick. He laughed and passed it off.

Some time later he called me to the hospital, as he wanted to have a talk with me. I found him lying on the bed with one leg in a cast. He asked me if I remembered what I had told him in regard to the matter of his being sick and the blessing it might be to him. I told him I did. "Well," he said, "I am not really sick, and I have no special pain. I had a condition that made it necessary for me to have the leg broken and reset, and now I am in a cast and will have to remain for some time. I have been doing some thinking. There are times when the leg itches most annoyingly, and there is nothing I can do about it. I would give a good deal if I could only scratch it, but because of the cast I cannot. Then the nurse will laugh at me and say that I will not die of itching. No, I won't die; but I tell you, at times I am most miserable. I think that when I get up again I will be a little more understanding with my patients." He was.

Time for Reflection

We can think of other doctors who need the same kind of treatment. And we can think of some preachers and teachers and officials and husbands and wives who would greatly profit by a few weeks on their backs with enough pain to keep them awake and thinking. Thinking on the sickbed is good for both body and soul. It may be that the reader as well as the writer could also benefit.

Sickness is an excellent time for reflection. The world is too much with us. We need time for taking an inventory of ourselves; but in the busy days of activity we have little time for this, or rather, we do not take time for it.

Men that never before gave serious thought to their relation to God may on the sick-bed find the time they need for introspection. Pain is thought-provoking.

These considerations lead us to the conviction that sickness may serve some good purpose and is not always only evil. Many a man has found God through pain.

For the Christian, sickness may be a precious experience. He knows that God loves him, and that it is not to torment him that he is laid low, but that God has some purpose in permitting him to suffer. He knows that when the test is over he will be able to say with Job, "He knoweth the way that I take: when He hath tried me, I shall come forth as gold." Job 23:10.

Let us sum up some of the ways in which a Christian may derive benefit from a period of enforced idleness.

1. Time to think. For this first time in a long while he has time to think. He has felt the need of this repeatedly, but has been so busy with other people and their difficulties that he has neglected to think of himself and his needs. Now he has the time he has always wanted.

2. Time to pray and meditate unhurriedly. He has felt the need of this, also, and promised himself that he *would* take time out for this. But always something has come in the way. But now at last he can be alone with God. He feels the need of getting better acquainted with his Maker. Now is the opportunity.

3. Sickness makes a Christian appreciate his friends more than ever. He never knew he had so many; but now even those whom he thought did not care whether he was sick or not, come to visit him, and some bring flowers and say kind words. The whole world seems a little better.

4. He has always been independent and spurned help from others. Now he finds that he cannot help himself; that he must depend on others even for a glass of water.

He learns that he is not self-sufficient, but helpless as a babe. He is in a new role, and he profits from it.

5. A mellow spirit. He thinks of the many times he has been impatient with the inefficiency of others; how he has used harsh and biting words and wounded sensitive souls, who probably did the best they were capable of. Now his spirit is being mellowed. He decides to be kinder, more understanding, and to show a true Christian spirit at all times. God is having him in school.

6. He learns that he is not indispensable. He always imagined that he did more than his share of the work and that things would go to pieces if he were not there. It hurts his pride to discover that he is not as important as he thought he was and that men can get along without him. To learn this is good for the soul.

Elijah was a good man and did a good work. But he came to the point where he considered himself indispensable. He felt sorry for God as he thought he was the only man left to do the work. 1 Kings 19:10, 14. God assured him, however, that this was not the case. He had yet seven thousand others who were faithful and could be used. Verse 18. It is good for a man who thinks he is unexpendable to be placed on the side lines for a while. It gives him a better view of his own importance, or lack of it.

If any man was ever indispensable, it was Paul. Yet, at the very time that it seemed impossible to continue the work without him, the Lord removed him, and Paul spent years in prison. Not that the Lord did not love him. He did. But the church needed to learn to trust in God and not in man.

7. A man's sickness may be a blessing to others who thus get an opportunity to develop talents that have been largely unused. Unsuspected abilities are discovered, and

men are given an opportunity to grow. This may be a by-product of sickness, but it is an important one.

When Paul was put in prison, he wrote about brethren who, "waxing confident by my bonds, are much more bold to speak the word without fear." Philippians 1:14. With Paul out of active service these men felt the responsibility of carrying on and perhaps experienced new freedom and boldness since their preaching would not now be compared with Paul's.

8. Sickness teaches a man to appreciate more than ever the many privileges that have been his, but are now denied him: meeting with others of like faith in Sabbath school and worship, in prayer meeting and social activities, at the Lord's table and the ordinance of service, in camp meeting and other gatherings. He longs for the time when he can again be with them, and still more for the great meeting beyond.

9. The greatest blessing that comes to a Christian on his sickbed is the conviction that God loves him and is preparing him to do a greater service, or, if He thinks best, to let him sleep in the grave until the Life-giver shall come. In either case he is in the hand of God and prays that God's will be done. In that conviction he can rest, assured that God knows best.

Having come to this conclusion, he is content and ready to say from the heart, "Thy will be done." That will may be rest from his labors, or it may be restoration to health and strength. We are assured that in many cases God is waiting for the sick one to come to the point where he has "faith to be healed" (Acts 14:9), faith to realize that he is sick for no other reason than that "the works of God should be made manifest in him" (John 9:3).

Instead, therefore, of considering sickness an affliction, it may be life's greatest opportunity to do what we have never had time to do before. Now we have that quietness and aloneness which is necessary for any great achievement. Sickness may be one of the greatest and most rewarding privileges of life. Let all, therefore, take courage.

Is Sickness a "Privilege"?

It might be well if we could come to look on sickness and pain as a privilege, an opportunity, rather than something to be endured and dreaded. Paul considered suffering a privilege and even a cause for rejoicing. Hear him say to his converts: "Unto you it is given in the behalf of Christ, not only to believe on Him, but also to suffer for His sake." Philippians 1:29. "I take pleasure in infirmities, in reproaches, in necessities, in persecutions, in distresses for Christ's sake: for when I am weak, then am I strong." 2 Corinthians 12:10.

We doubt that Paul enjoyed suffering as such. But when he thought of what it would do for him and others, he rejoiced in it. He needed patience. And he knew that tribulation would help develop it. So he did not complain. He rejoiced.

Paul learned that suffering was not necessarily an affliction, but one of God's means of developing character. This viewpoint changes suffering from a calamity to an opportunity. We may then rest quietly, knowing that God is doing a work for us that needs to be done. Thus sickness becomes one of God's means for our salvation, and if we co-operate with Him, it will not be time wasted in bed, but precious seasons with God that will mean much to us on our way to the kingdom. So do not fret because of sickness. *Use it.* Life will be richer ever after because of your enforced idleness. We may make greater strides toward the kingdom by lying on our back than in the busy activities of life.

18

Sickness and Prayer

IF GOD does not answer our prayer after a reasonable wait, are we to believe that God does not wish to grant our request, bow in submission to His will, and discontinue praying about the matter? Or are we to conclude that God is testing us to see if we are really in earnest, and wants us to continue praying?

The answer to these questions depends upon several factors, and cannot be decided by a simple Yes or No. Let us consider some of the factors involved, particularly with reference to suffering and healing.

One who is afflicted should first of all attempt to ascertain if he is suffering because of transgression of the laws of health and life, and is reaping the results of what he has sown. If he finds himself guilty, he should immediately discontinue the practices that have brought on his condition. This is a *must*. W cannot expect God to save us from the results of our folly, if we refuse to mend our ways. Nor are we to change our ways merely for the sake of getting well. A higher principle should motivate us: that of doing right because it *is* right, and not merely that we may benefit by it.

We know that God is love and does not want any to

suffer needlessly. If He therefore hesitates in granting us healing, He has good reasons for doing so. One who keeps in close touch with God will know these reasons.

If a Christian thoroughly repents of his sins and of those things which have brought on his sickness, asking God for forgiveness and healing, and no healing comes, what is he to do next? He is to wait patiently for God. He is to remember that only under extraordinary circumstances does God interfere with the orderly processes of nature. The conditions that brought on the sickness were a long time developing, and the healing time may be lengthened proportionately. God always works along the lines He has laid down and in harmony with the laws He has ordained. Unless some emergency arises and God sees fit to perform a miracle, the ordinary laws of nature will be permitted to work.

Suffering and Repentance

It should be had in mind that the results of transgression are not necessarily a direct punishment inflicted by God, but the natural results of man's own acts. They are the *wages* of sin which he has earned. God does not kill a man because he drinks carbolic acid. The man kills himself. The punishment for violating the laws of health and of nature is inherent in the transgression and is not the result of a direct act of God. The man intent on suicide who pulls the trigger might pray God to prevent the bullet from entering his body, but such prayer would be in vain. Yet it would be no more inconsistent than to ask God to prevent the harvest from the seed sown. "Whatsoever a man soweth, that shall he also reap." Galatians 6:7.

Can nothing be done for the man who realizes that he is suffering justly for what he has done, but is repentant?

Yes, much can be done. The very fact that he under-stands why he is afflicted is in itself a great gain. He sees the justice of God, and life takes on new meaning for him. He does not blame God; he blames himself. He is at peace with God and quietly asks God to begin the healing proc-ess in his body. He does not ask for exemption from the punishment he has brought on himself; he asks for grace to bear it. He does not ask the surgeon to stop in the midst of an operation, but wants him to finish it and to remove every trace of corruption that might bring on a new attack if not removed. He desires healing, but he wants the sur-geon to do his work first. So he quietly waits upon God. God will give him grace, and the process of restoration will begin as soon as the man is ready for it. It may take time, but God is performing no less a miracle in the slow process of healing than in an instantaneous miracle. Won-derful is the body's power of recuperation, and when a man co-operates with God, virtual miracles may be ac-complished.

Let the sick man take courage. He may have brought on the sickness himself and may feel that he has amply deserved the affliction that has come to him. But let him be of good cheer. Let him pray—pray as never before. And God will hear. He has ways of accomplishing in a short time what ordinarily would take years; and when He can do this without violating His own laws, He will do it. But He must have the co-operation of the sick and must make sure not to go too fast lest the lesson fail to make the impression that it should. In this way the sick one may pass through an experience with God that amply repays him for the time spent on the sickbed. He will thank God for the affliction that brought him nearer to his Lord.

God hears and answers the prayers of those who suffer,

even when they are suffering justly. He is reluctant to punish, and the moment one turns to Him, He receives him with open arms. The story of how the prodigal son's father received the returning son is to the point. Luke 15:20-24. God does not wait one moment to start the healing process after the man has repented.

The time of sickness and recovery is God's opportunity to help and instruct the sick. In the night season God can speak to him, and he begins to see the divine philosophy of affliction and healing. He understands that God is taking him in hand and is teaching him needed lessons, and he gladly accepts them. From a full heart he prays, "Lord, I am suffering justly. I have transgressed and done evil, and I am reaping what I have sown. I have no complaint to make; rather, I am so thankful for being called while there is still hope. I am happy that I have been permitted to know Thee and Thy ways better. I believe, Lord, I have learned my lesson, and that if Thou shouldest see best to heal me, Thy will be done. I am not asking for speedy healing, Lord, unless it be Thy will. I am content; I am submissive. And if it is best that I remain on my sickbed, I am ready. I have faith in Thee. I resign myself willingly into Thy hands."

Such a prayer God loves to hear. It gives Him a free hand. The sick one does not demand that God work a miracle; he humbly asks that God's will be done, and promises to be satisfied whatever comes. God now has a man who has learned his lesson and who has sufficient faith to leave his case with God. Such is a man after God's heart.

Thus far our discussion has dealt with those who are conscious of sin and know they are suffering justly. But there are other dear souls who have no such consciousness and are not aware of any sin that could have brought on their affliction. What are such to do when they find them-selves afflicted?

The Lesson for Paul

It was not until Paul had prayed the third time for God to remove the thorn that he found the reason for his afflic-tion. It was not because he had sinned; the thorn was a precautionary measure taken by God to keep him from threatening pride. Paul had a tendency to pride, but did not fully recognize his danger until God revealed it to him. Then he saw and acknowledged it. He confessed that God had "given to me a thorn in the flesh, the mes-senger of Satan to buffet me, lest I should be exalted above measure." 2 Corinthians 12:7. He prayed no more to have the thorn removed, but thanked God for it and said, "Most gladly therefore will I rather glory in my infirmities, that the power of Christ may rest upon me." Verse 9.

This may explain why some people are afflicted, yet not conscious of any known sin. They may have a thorn in the flesh, and if so they may ask God humbly for the reason. The thorn may be the means of their salvation; but, not being fully aware of their need, they chafe under the affliction and ask God to remove it. Let such seek the Lord with all their heart. God has promised, "Ye shall seek Me, and find Me, when ye shall search for Me with all your heart." Jeremiah 29:13.

Should those pray who are afflicted and are not sure of the reason? Most assuredly. They are not necessarily to pray to have the affliction removed, but humbly to pray to learn its reason and the lesson, and thus in submission find God's strength "made perfect in weakness." It may be that they, with Paul, will find that they need the expe-rience, and should not pray to have the affliction removed unless God clearly indicates that this is His will.

19

Prayer for Healing

THE passage most often quoted as authorizing prayer for the sick is found in the epistle of James and reads as follows: "Is any among you afflicted? let him pray. Is any merry? let him sing psalms. Is any sick among you? let him call for the elders of the church; and let them pray over him, anointing him with oil in the name of the Lord: and the prayer of faith shall save the sick, and the Lord shall raise him up; and if he have committed sins, they shall be forgiven him. Confess your faults one to another, and pray one for another, that ye may be healed. The effectual fervent prayer of a righteous man availeth much." James 5:13-16.

These verses have been subject to much dispute. Some hold that prayer for healing is no longer necessary, since we have well-trained physicians and surgeons as well as good hospitals giving efficient service. Under these conditions there is no need of appealing to heaven for help which we can supply ourselves. Others take the position that healing is as much a part of the gospel as preaching, and that God intends that the two shall go hand in hand until the end of time.

As believers in the Bible and the divine commission to

preach the gospel to every creature, we hold that it is our work to harmonize as nearly as possible with the pattern given us in the example and teaching of Jesus. This teaching includes the instruction given by James, wherein he counsels us that in the case of sickness the elders of the church are to be called to pray for the one who is sick, anointing him with oil in the name of the Lord, and the prayer of faith shall save the sick. Let us carefully review the exhortation which James gives.

James Speaks

"Is any among you afflicted? let him pray." The afflicted here mentioned may be any person who has one of the many ailments that beset men, which are not ordinarily fatal, but annoying and often painful. For such, James says, "let him pray."

God is interested in all that concerns us, and we may come to Him even with what may seem trivial matters. That He asks us to come is in itself significant, for we cannot believe that God would invite us if all He had in mind was to ignore our plea. While permission to approach Him might not imply an unconditional promise to heal, it does show God's interest in our welfare and certainly indicates that He is predisposed in our favor. That we may come to Him with our minor afflictions also shows us that we are not to wait until some severe sickness or calamity overtakes us. We may appeal to Him at any time and in any matter whatsoever.

"Is any merry? let him sing psalms." There are times when all is well and we feel like singing. James advises us to sing, but suggests that we sing psalms. Singing releases pent-up feelings and is an excellent way to express our joy. But James says we should be careful *what* we sing and calls our attention to psalms as a safe way to express ourselves and yet retain our hold upon God. How often in an unguarded moment some little ditty comes to mind, or a snatch of a catchy tune, and before we are aware of what we are doing we are humming some popular song not becoming to a Christian. Paul's advice is to sing "with grace in your hearts to the Lord," using "psalms and hymns and spiritual songs." Colossians 3:16. After having received many stripes and being cast into prison, "at midnight Paul and Silas prayed, and sang praises unto God." Acts 16:25. Singing praise to God is acceptable under all circumstances where song is called for.

"Is any sick among you? let him call for the elders." This does not refer to a minor affliction as in verse 13, but to a more serious condition. The sick may already have prayed, but as no relief comes he feels the need of having others join him, and he calls for the elders of the church.

By "elders" are not here meant only the elected elders of the church, but men of experience in whom the sick has confidence and who will gladly respond when called upon. It is not official position which qualifies them, but an unction from on high, faith, consecration, humility, godly life, strict integrity, and a good report from them that are without. If they have official position, so much the better; but this is not necessary.

"Let him call." This statement indicates that the sick initiates the call. It must be his personal desire, and no pressure is to be brought on him to have the elders called. It must be of his own free will, and no one else is to take the responsibility to issue the call. However, there may be those who are too sick to call, or who do not feel worthy of having the elders come, or who are too reticent to make their wishes known. In such cases it is proper that others step in. In all these matters let Christian tact and courtesy be exercised.

We have known zealous and well-meaning church members who have asked the elders to come when there was no call from the sick and he was unaware of what was being done. This may cause embarrassment when he is unprepared for a visit. The sick should first be consulted and given time for preparation. The same holds true of the elders. They should be notified in time. Not all may be ready to come on a moment's notice. At times there are necessary arrangements and adjustments that must be made, as well as counsel with the other elders.

"Let them pray over him." This suggests the little group of elders seeking God together and praying for the sick. The wording indicates that more than one should pray. In its strict interpretation it would seem that all should pray, but this is possible only where the group is small and no one prays at length. Long prayers, or many prayers, are wearisome, do not profit anyone, and might easily have an adverse influence on the sick.

The Primary Question

Let no one think that he will be heard because he prays loud and long, or uses a "holy tone" or whining voice different from his usual manner of speaking. Oratorical expressions, high-sounding exclamations, pious platitudes, affected play on the emotions, and dictating to God have no place in prayer. Let prayers be offered in simplicity and sincerity, with deep, abiding faith in God and His promises. There are occasions where the Spirit of God takes full control and hearts are melted. At such times let no one interfere with God's workings. But professional emotions and easy tears are not to be indulged in. Souls are at stake; a life is hanging in the balance. Let all be done with appropriate solemnity and holy decorum.

We have stated elsewhere that effective prayer must be

in accordance with God's will. It is therefore of the utmost importance that the elders ascertain what is the will of God in any particular case. The paramount question is not that of healing, but the ascertainment of God's will. This means that the elders should counsel and pray together before they approach the sick for prayer. Are they all agreed that the time has come for prayer? Are all agreed that it is God's undoubted will that the sick be healed? Is it His will that he be healed *now?* Will it be for God's glory and for the good of the sick? Has he learned the lessons God has for him in this sickness? Has he abstained from, or does he now promise to abstain from, every evil habit? Does God desire instant healing, or will He use nature's slower way? Is it possible that God may not think it best to heal at all, but that the time has come for the sick to rest from his labors and sleep till the Lord comes? Is the sick willing to leave all in the hands of God? Will he cheerfully accept God's way and will? Is he ready to say, Thy will be done?

Such preliminary counsel and prayer among the elders are necessary before they pray for the sick. They need to pray for themselves first. They need to come into agreement among themselves in regard to what they are to ask. Says Christ, "If two of you shall agree on earth as touching anything that they shall ask, it shall be done for them of My Father which is in heaven." Matthew 18:19. This promise is not to be discounted. It will be fulfilled as are all other promises of God.

But this promise must not be interpreted independently of and apart from other statements of Holy Writ. Every prayer to be heard must be according to the will of God, or the prayer will be in vain. It is a most solemn thing to pray for and anoint the sick. It must not be done lightly and without preparation on the part of those who pray.

They must be in harmony. The counsel and prayer of the elders before they pray for the sick is an important part of God's plan and must not be omitted.

We cannot emphasize too often that it is imperative for all who pray and expect their prayers to be answered, to pray according to God's will. We sometimes are so anxious to have our will done that we forget that God is wiser than we, that however much we want a certain thing, it may not be for the best, and that God knows better than we do. We are likely to command God to do what we want done and forget that it might do much harm if our prayers were answered. It should be had in mind that there are times when God lets us have our way to teach us a lesson, as when Israel "lusted exceedingly in the wilderness, and tempted God in the desert. And He gave them their request; but sent leanness into their soul." Psalm 106:14, 15. We must be particularly careful in our prayers for the sick lest we pray for what we ought not to.

"Anointing him with oil." When the elders have prayed that God's will be done, and the sick has fully agreed, he is ready for the anointing. The oil is symbolic of the Holy Spirit, and the anointing constitutes a sealing of the heart to God, a dedication, a consecration. Exodus 28:41; Acts 10:38. The elders pray to the Father in the name of the Son, and the Holy Spirit seals the compact. The Three Powers of heaven are present.

"The prayer of faith shall save the sick." This is a definite promise. "If we confess our sins, He is faithful and just to forgive us our sins, and to cleanse us from all unrighteousness." 1 John 1:9. When the conditions are fulfilled, the prayer of faith shall save the sick. He has given himself fully into the hands of God, the elders have anointed him with oil in the name of the Lord, and now God fulfills His part. "The prayer of faith shall save the sick." This is the first of the three results of prayer here named. The others are: "The Lord shall raise him up," and "If he have committed sins, they shall be forgiven him."

The first promise that the prayer of faith shall save the sick is the most precious and important of the three. Whether the sick is healed or not is of less importance than the saving of the soul. This is the first promise. Even before healing is mentioned comes this comforting message to the sick that he shall be saved.

This salvation is not brought about by the prayers of the elders apart from the co-operation of the sick. No man or group of men can save anyone else, however much they may pray, unless the sinner himself turns to God and fulfills the condition of forgiveness. Says God, "though these three men, Noah, Daniel, and Job, were in it, they should deliver but their own souls by their righteousness, saith the Lord God." Ezekiel 14:14. In forgiveness of sin, in salvation, the man himself must co-operate; and as he does so, the promise is sure: the prayer of faith shall save the sick. We need not emphasize that the faith here spoken of is not faith in the *prayer* they are uttering, but faith in *God*. Faith in one's own prayer is only faith in one's self. It is faith in God that counts.

"The Lord shall raise him up." Some have taken this to mean that if the sick is not healed, but dies, the promise will yet be fulfilled; for the Lord will raise him up from the dead in the resurrection of the great day. While this is true, the evident meaning of the text is that God will heal him and raise him up from his sickbed. This promise is as sure as the one that the Lord will save the sick; but like every other promise, it is conditioned upon compliance with God's will and limited by God's appointments. We can appreciate God's power and willingness to raise a man from his sickbed and restore him to health and strength. But we cannot believe that God will do this repeatedly so the man will never die. God does not do this because in His wisdom He has appointed unto men once to die, and men must keep that appointment. Hebrews 9:27. So, however much a man may pray, and however much others may pray for him, unless God does a special miracle and translates him to heaven without seeing death, the time will come when prayer for healing and health and life will avail no more.

Thus we can understand that good men may pray for the healing of a good man and not be heard. Yet in the larger sense their prayer is heard, for, being dedicated to God, they have added to their prayer, "Thy will be done." That is how Paul could say of Christ, "When He had offered up prayers and supplications with strong crying and tears unto Him that was able to save Him from death, and was heard in that He feared; ... yet learned He obedience by the things which He suffered." Hebrews 5:7, 8. Christ was not exempt from drinking the cup though He prayed three times to be delivered; yet we are told that His prayer was heard. He added, "Thy will be done," and having added this, His will was the same as God's.

We need not lose faith because prayer does not bring life and health to someone we love. God knows best, and we must leave the matter with Him. But we are persuaded that we are not taking advantage of God's promises as we should and that because of our lack of faith "many are weak and sickly among you, and many sleep." 1 Corinthians 11:30.

A Sobering Thought

It is a sobering thought that there may be those among us today who are sick for no other reason than that "the works of God should be made manifest," as was the case of the young man who had been blind from birth. They are waiting for someone to come with enough faith in God so that His works may be made manifest. John 9:3. It is a disturbing fact that some are sick and weakly among us because we have not fully appropriated the power and blessing there are in the ordinances of the Lord's house. 1 Corinthians 11:23-30. It is time that God's people claim all the gifts which God has set in the church, and not only one or two. 1 Corinthians 12:28. We are counseled to "come behind in no gift; waiting for the coming of our Lord Jesus Christ." 1 Corinthians 1:7. Is it not time for the church to come up to the help of the Lord against the mighty? Judges 5:23. But let all beware of fanaticism.

"Sins . . . shall be forgiven him." This promise is as sure as the others and is based on the same conditions: repentance and confession. "If we confess our sins, He is faithful and just to forgive us our sins, and to cleanse us from all unrighteousness." 1 John 1:9. That is the condition. John is not here propounding a new doctrine. Men may set up their confessionals and promise forgiveness to such as come to them. But God does not recognize or authorize such man-made arrangements. His invitation is, "Come unto *Me,* all ye that labor and are heavy-laden, and *I* will give you rest." Matthew 11:28.

Christ has not abdicated and turned His work over to fallible men. No man has a right to invite men to come to him and receive absolution. Yet, while Christ is performing His office in the sanctuary in heaven, an opposing power has set up its sanctuary on earth and is inviting men to come to it. And they come. Paul speaks of this when he says that before the Lord comes, there shall come "a falling away first," so that the man of sin may be revealed, "the son of perdition; who opposeth and exalteth himself above all that is called God, or that is worshiped; so that he as God sitteth in the temple of God, showing himself that he is God." 2 Thessalonians 2:3, 4.

"Confess your faults one to another." We are to confess our sins to God, our faults one to another. In neither case are we commanded to confess to a priest. We are, indeed, to confess to man, but the man to whom we are to confess is the man we have wronged. If I have sinned against Brother Jones, I am not to confess to Brother Smith. This is axiomatic.

We are to confess our faults *one to another*. If I am to confess my sins to a priest, then he is to confess his sins to me. If he gives me absolution, then I am to give him the same. Such is the absurdity of man-made ordinances.

"Pray one for another." Prayer is a mutual privilege and responsibility. I am to pray for my brother, and he is to pray for me. We are on an equal footing in prayer. Pray for one another "that ye may be healed." It is not that "he" may be healed, but "ye." God recognizes, and so are we also to recognize, that though we may pray for another, we ourselves need healing. This should make us humble as we pray.

"The effectual fervent prayer of a righteous man availeth much." This is an interesting and important statement. The two words "effectual" and "fervent" are translated from one Greek word, *energo,* from which our word "energy" is derived. What does James mean when he says this kind of prayer by a righteous man availeth much? He does not explain this, but cites the case of Elijah to illustrate it.

For many years this illustration worried me. Elijah was a mighty man of God, and how could the fact that God heard him be any encouragement to me? I was neither righteous nor great.

I noted that God said Elijah was a man of like passions as we. But that I could not believe. There must be some mistake in using Elijah as a type.

But then I discovered that Elijah also had his weak points. After the wonderful day on the mount where he stood alone against all the priests of Baal and Astarte, he basely ran away because Jezebel threatened him. He could stand against all the prophets of Baal, but could not stand against one woman. And his running away would likely have serious consequences for Israel. For Israel had turned to God, and a wonderful revival took place after Elijah had been answered with fire from heaven. It had been amply demonstrated that Elijah's God was stronger than Jezebel's prophets and their gods. But now that Elijah had fled from Jezebel, the people could draw no other conclusion than that, after all, Jezebel's gods were the greater and more powerful, and Israel might now all apostatize and turn from God to serve Baal.

It was a most serious mistake for Elijah to run away. But did God cast him aside? As he and Elisha were walking together, "there appeared a chariot of fire, and horses of fire, and parted them both asunder; and Elijah went up by a whirlwind into heaven." 2 Kings 2:11.

It is to be noted that God mercifully hid from the people the fact that Elijah ran away, so the feared apostasy did not take place.

This makes clear why God uses Elijah as a type. We may have made serious mistakes as did Elijah. Despite this, God may bless us as we pray. He heard Elijah; He will hear us.

20

8 - 82

Paul and Suffering

IN MANY respects Paul was a remarkable man. God called him "a chosen vessel unto Me, to bear My name before the Gentiles, and kings, and the children of Israel." Acts 9:15. Immediately upon his conversion God showed him "how great things he must suffer for My name's sake." Verse 16. As suffering was to be a part of God's program for Paul, he came to look upon it as a privilege. Said he, "Unto you it is given in the behalf of Christ, not only to believe on Him, but also to suffer for His sake." Philippians 1:29.

Peter told the believers, "If, when ye do well, and suffer for it, ye take it patiently, this is acceptable with God." 1 Peter 2:20. Paul took the same ground in Romans 12:12, where he told the saints to be "patient in tribulation." While both agreed that to be patient in tribulation is "acceptable with God," Paul took an advanced position when he said that as for himself he had learned not only to be patient in suffering, but to *rejoice in* his sufferings for them. Colossians 1:24.

Few have advanced that far. Most think that they do well if they are patient in suffering. And God says that this is acceptable. But Paul wanted to go further, following Christ's admonition in Matthew 5:11, 12: "Blessed are ye, when men shall revile you, and persecute you, and shall say all manner of evil against you falsely, for My sake. Rejoice, and be exceeding glad: for great is your reward in heaven: for so persecuted they the prophets which were before you."

Christ "took our infirmities, and bare our sicknesses." Matthew 8:17. He was tempted in all points "like as we are, yet without sin." Hebrews 4:15. As "He Himself hath suffered being tempted, He is able to succor them that are tempted." Hebrews 2:18. These trials came to Christ "that He might be a merciful and faithful High Priest." Verse 17.

As Paul learned that Christ's sufferings enabled Him to sympathize with others and understand their sufferings, he desired to be permitted to suffer with Christ. Thus he also would be able, when others suffered, to understand and help them.

Paul's Sufferings

The more Paul thought of suffering, not as affliction but as a means of preparation to help others, the more he desired to go all the way with Christ and suffer as He had suffered. To the Corinthians he wrote that God "comforteth us in all our tribulation, that we may be able to comfort them which are in any trouble, by the comfort wherewith we ourselves are comforted of God. For as the sufferings of Christ abound in us, so our consolation also aboundeth by Christ. And whether we be afflicted, it is for your consolation and salvation, which is effectual in the enduring of the same sufferings which we also suffer: or whether we be comforted, it is for your consolation and salvation." 2 Corinthians 1:4-6.

Paul considered his sufferings vicarious, as were

Christ's. He did not suffer for himself; he suffered for others. And his sufferings would benefit the saints. As he suffered and was comforted by God, he was enabled to comfort others with the same comfort which he had received.

We suppose that Paul was sensitive to pain as are other men. He did not enjoy pain for pain's sake. It was only as pain served a definite purpose in helping others that he was interested in it. If he could do others good by suffering, he was not only willing but anxious to suffer.

Paul discovered that he could do this. When some afflicted saint learned that Paul had had an experience similar to his, a bond of sympathy and understanding was immediately established, and the poor soul took courage. He could at least learn to bear with patience the tribulation over which Paul rejoiced.

The Thorn in the Flesh

Paul stated, "I have learned, in whatsoever state I am, therewith to be content." Philippians 4:11. So when he found himself in prison with a lacerated back from which the blood ran down, he began to think how this particular experience would be of help to him. Then "Paul and Silas prayed, and sang praises unto God: and the prisoners heard them." Acts 16:25. Doubtless the other inmates wondered if these men had lost their minds, for who had ever heard a person singing for joy after being beaten with "many stripes"?

Paul wanted to follow Christ all the way. As Christ had suffered, so Paul wanted to suffer. As He went to the cross, so Paul wanted to be "made comformable unto His death." Philippians 3:10. As Christ in all things was made like unto His brethren, so Paul wanted in all things to be made like unto Christ.

Paul was greatly beloved of God, yet all his life he had to live with a thorn in the flesh, which he frankly confesses was given to keep him humble. Paul would not have needed to make this confession. While we might suspect that the many revelations he had would tend to make him proud, we would not be sure that this was the case unless he had expressly said so. Twice in the same verse he stated that the thorn was given him "lest I should be exalted above measure." 2 Corinthians 12:7. He called the thorn "the messenger of Satan to buffet me." Paul gave us this information to let us know that God is no respecter of persons and that there is no difference of treatment because of position.

While we do not know what this thorn was, we may be certain that it was a painful affliction or Paul would not call it a thorn. God did not remove the thorn, but gave him grace to bear it, and from a full heart Paul could say, "Most gladly therefore will I rather glory in my infirmities, that the power of Christ may rest upon me." Verse 9.

From these considerations we learn that when affliction comes to one of the saints, God has His purpose in it and that He is working out some plan that will eventually be for our good. Satan will always be present trying to discourage and harass the saint. But if the sick will co-operate with God, Satan's attempt will only strengthen him in his determination to do right at all cost, and he will be the stronger for the conflict. Thus it may be with every assault of Satan.

This same principle I saw illustrated in a school I was once connected with. There were two teachers of mathematics in the school, a young man and a man of more experience. The younger man was asked to teach a subject which he had not taught before. The school furnished a teacher's manual, which would save the teacher much time and work. The older teacher kept the book from the younger teacher, causing him to have a difficult time. But without the manual he had to study harder, with the result that when the year was ended he was a much better teacher than if he had received help. He became so proficient in his field that in due time he became the head of the department, something that might not have occurred if he had not had to do his own studying. What was meant to hamper him turned out to be a help.

Satan Is Happy

Satan would like to torment us and is happy when he can bring us into difficult positions. But in doing so, he is really working against himself, for "tribulation worketh patience," the very virtue God would have us develop. For this reason Paul could say, "We glory in tribulations also: knowing that tribulation worketh patience." Romans 5:3. Thus when Satan throws rocks in our path, God makes them into steppingstones if we work with Him.

Sickness may be a disheartening and discouraging experience as we consider the grief and sorrow it brings to loved ones. If in addition to this we fear that God has forsaken or forgotten us, and that He does not seem to hear our prayers, it may be a most distressing and faith-trying hour. Trust in God dims, faith in Him wavers, financial involvements dismay us, and we wonder if God really has forsaken us. We go through the deep waters. The lamp of hope burns low.

But let the sick and discouraged soul look to God. He still lives and loves. He may let dark clouds envelop us temporarily; but behind the cloud is the sunshine of God's love. God is at every sickbed, ready to help as needed. Cling by faith to the promises of God. Search your hearts for sins of which you may not be fully aware. Be honest with yourself and with your God. Confess where needed. Restore where restitution is possible. Clear the King's highway; make straight paths for your feet. If you thus seek God and ask Him to reveal to you any unsuspected weakness, He will come near.

If after this thorough and honest self-examination you are not conscious of sin, or if you have sinned and confessed, then thank God for His forgiveness and love, and by faith rejoice that God has accepted you, and ask Him to cleanse you from *every* sin. As you do this, new hope and peace will come into your soul, and being perfectly resigned to God, you may from the heart say, "Lord, Thy will be done." You have done what you could, and God will do His part.

21

Prayer and the Gift
of Healing

OF JESUS it is written that He "went about all Galilee, teaching in their synagogues, and preaching the gospel of the kingdom, and healing all manner of sickness and all manner of disease among the people." Matthew 4:23. When He had selected the Twelve, "He gave them power against unclean spirits, to cast them out, and to heal all manner of sickness and all manner of disease." Matthew 10:1. "And they went out, and preached that men should repent. And they cast out many devils, and anointed with oil many that were sick, and healed them." Mark 6:12, 13. He "gave them power and authority over all devils, and to cure diseases." "And they departed, and went through the towns, preaching the gospel, and healing everywhere." Luke 9:1, 6.

These references show that healing is an integral part of the gospel. As Christ and the apostles preached repentance from sin, they also touched men's bodies and made them whole. In doing this, Christ honored the body and taught men that religion is not confined to certain theological concepts, but is intended for the whole man, and that all might have healing of bodily infirmities as well as forgiveness of sin.

(153)

The gift of healing is one of the gifts of the Spirit (1 Corinthians 12:9, 28), and is to be distinguished from prayer for healing. All Christians have the privilege to pray for healing; but the gift of healing is given to but few to use in their ministry and is accompanied by the gift of discernment, which is necessary that they may know who is worthy of healing and who have the necessary faith.

As the disciples exercised this gift and people saw healing taking place before their eyes, naturally the news spread quickly, and multitudes assembled to see miracles being done. This provided an audience for the healer, which is one of the objects God has in mind in giving men the gift.

Christ used this method in His work. When He commissioned the seventy to go out, He sent them "into every city and place, whither He Himself would come." Luke 10:1. They constituted an advance army, heralding the fact that Christ would soon come to their city, perhaps even announcing the time when He would come. They were to "heal the sick that are therein, and say unto them, The kingdom of God is come nigh unto you." Verse 9. As they came to a town, it is easy to imagine the stir their arrival would cause. They had power not only to heal the sick, but also to cast out devils, "to tread on serpents and scorpions, and over all the power of the enemy." Verse 19. When they healed the sick and drove out devils they did not take the honor to themselves for these miracles, but gladly acknowledged, "The devils are subject unto us through Thy name." Verse 17. For every healing that took place, Christ was given credit, and thus the way was prepared for Him when He should shortly arrive. The people rightly wondered, If the servants could do such wonderful miracles, what might not the Master do

when He should come? With such an advertising van-
guard the multitudes were ready for Christ when He
arrived.

God's Purpose

The gift of healing served as a strong factor in spreading the news of the gospel to many who would not otherwise be attracted by an unknown preacher just passing
through the town, and as a means of restoring health.
Furthermore, it served as a sign of God's approval of the
men He used, "God also bearing them witness, both with
signs and wonders, and with divers miracles, and gifts of
the Holy Ghost, according to His own will." Hebrews
2:4. It was God's testimony to the credentials of His
servants; it was His seal placed upon the faithful laborer,
giving him standing in the eyes of the people as approved
of God. In Christ's day the work of the seventy was a
vital factor in the success of the Master's mission. It gave
Him an enthusiastic and respectful hearing in many
places where His visit of a day or two would otherwise
have been insufficient to accomplish what He wished.

Prayer and Gift of Healing

Working as a healer, Christ did not pray publicly. In
healing the centurion's servant, we do not find Christ
praying or saying anything to the centurion. But "they
that were sent, returning to the house, found the servant
whole that had been sick." Luke 7:10.

When Christ raised the widow's son from death, He
did not pray, but merely said, "Young man, I say unto
thee, Arise. And he that was dead sat up, and began to
speak." Verses 14, 15.

When Christ met the man who was "full of leprosy"
and who asked Christ to heal him, Jesus "put forth His

hand, and touched him, saying, I will: be thou clean. And immediately the leprosy departed from him." Luke 5: 12, 13.

To the man sick of the palsy Christ said, "Arise, and take up thy couch, and go into thine house." Verse 24. To the "spirit of an unclean devil" who possessed a man, Christ said, "Hold thy peace, and come out of him." Luke 4:33-35. At another time Christ "rebuked the unclean spirit, and healed the child." Luke 9:42. To the woman who "had a spirit of infirmity eighteen years," He said, "Woman, thou art loosed from thine infirmity." Luke 13:11, 12. To the ten lepers He said, "Go show yourselves unto the priests. And it came to pass, that, as they went, they were cleansed." Luke 17:14.

The disciples followed the same practice. To the lame man at the temple gate, Peter said, "In the name of Jesus Christ of Nazareth rise up and walk." Acts 3:6. Paul, healing "a certain man at Lystra, impotent in his feet, being a cripple from his mother's womb, who never had walked: . . . said with a loud voice, Stand upright on thy feet. And he leaped and walked." Acts 14:8-10.

To this custom of not praying at the time of healing, we find two exceptions: At the grave of Lazarus Jesus offered a brief prayer of thanks, stating that He did so on account of those who stood by. Then He cried, "Lazarus, come forth. And he that was dead came forth." John 11:43, 44. After the death of Dorcas, Peter put all the people out of the chamber "and kneeled down, and prayed; and turning him to the body said, Tabitha, arise. And she opened her eyes: and when she saw Peter, she sat up." Acts 9:40.

The common practice, therefore, seemed to be that whoever had the gift of healing spoke directly to the sick, and the person was healed. We can account for this on no other grounds than that the healer had such close contact with God that he could speak for God, knowing just what God wanted him to do. And that was what he proceeded to do. God reposed complete trust in him and gave him divine powers. He did not pray, Thy will be done. He knew already what was God's will, and God trusted him.

A study of the cases here mentioned shows that generally the healing had the effect of creating a widespread interest and that many were thus brought in close contact with the gospel by learning what it could do for men. The curiosity aroused was used by God to bring His message to the world. Thus the healing of the blind man recorded in the ninth chapter of John served to stir up the interest of the people as well as of the scribes, Pharisees, and priests. When Peter healed the man at the temple gate, "All the people ran together unto them in the porch that is called Solomon's." Acts 3:11. When Paul healed the lame man at Lystra, the people became so stirred up that they believed the gods had come down to them. Acts 14:11-18. God had means then of stirring up the people. He has means now.

False Miracles

We are told that Satan always attempts to imitate the work of God for the purpose of deceiving the people. When we, therefore, read that Satan will cause miracles to be wrought, and "the sick will be healed, and many undeniable wonders will be performed," we know that this will be because God's people will have received the power they should have had long ago. See *The Great Controversy,* page 588. As Satan cannot imitate without having something to imitate, we know that God's people will have the power promised the early church. Accordingly we read: "Miracles will be wrought, the sick will be healed, and signs and wonders will follow the believers."—*Ibid.*, p. 612.

"God hath set some in the church, first apostles, secondarily prophets, thirdly teachers, after that miracles, then gifts of healings, helps, governments, diversities of tongues." 1 Corinthians 12:28.

Some churches claim the gift of healings, others of diversities of tongues, others of prophets, others of apostles. We cannot believe that God intended that these gifts should be divided up among the different sects. Rather, God's church should have all of these, and not one or two. Is it not time that God's people awake and claim the powers God has for them?

The field is still open. While there are churches which claim to have certain gifts, it is doubtful that their claims will stand the test of investigation. And investigation there will surely be. When the time comes, God's church should be ready to step in and "take over," "God also bearing them witness, both with signs and wonders, and with divers miracles, and gifts of the Holy Ghost, according to His own will." Hebrews 2:4.

It is too late in the day to make excuses to the world for the lack of power in the church. We need to make our confession to God, to "be watchful, and strengthen the things which remain" (Revelation 3:2), and God will yet "restore to you the years that the locust hath eaten" (Joel 2:25).

22

Jesus and Prayer

IN HIS earth life Jesus ever kept in close touch with the Father. This might be expected, for from eternity They had been co-workers, and were one in planning both for creation and for redemption. Of Christ it is written, "The Lord possessed Me in the beginning of His way, before His works of old. I was set up from everlasting, from the beginning, or ever the earth was. . . . When He prepared the heavens, I was there. . . . I was by Him, as one brought up with Him." Proverbs 8:22-30.

God Himself bears this testimony: "Unto the Son He saith, Thy throne, O God, is for ever and ever: a scepter of righteousness is the scepter of Thy kingdom. . . . Thou, Lord, in the beginning hast laid the foundation of the earth; and the heavens are the works of Thine hands." Hebrews 1:8-10.

If any reader is perplexed over the statements just quoted, which attribute creation to both Father and Son, let him find the solution in Ephesians 3:9: "God, who created all things by Jesus Christ." And again, "To us there is but one God, the Father, of whom are all things, and we in Him; and one Lord Jesus Christ, by whom are all things, and we by Him." 1 Corinthians 8:6. Christ

(159)

and the Father worked together in the work of creation.

Having worked closely together in creation, They were now working closely together in that part of redemption which required Christ to come to this earth, and which would eventuate in His death on the cross. In all that Christ did on earth, He was guided by the pattern outlined in heaven, which was being communicated constantly to Him by the Father. "I came down from heaven, not to do Mine own will, but the will of Him that sent Me." John 6:38. "The Son can do nothing of Himself, but what He seeth the Father do: for what things soever He doeth, these also doeth the Son likewise." John 5:19.

Even the doctrine Jesus taught, He had derived from the Father. "Jesus answered them, and said, My doctrine is not Mine, but His that sent Me." John 7:16. "And the word which ye hear is not Mine, but the Father's which sent Me." John 14:24. "As My Father hath taught Me, I speak these things." John 8:28. The Father "showeth Him all things that Himself doeth," and "what things soever He doeth, these also doeth the Son likewise." "I do always those things that please Him." John 5:20, 19; 8:29. The prophet had said of Christ, "The Lord God hath given me the tongue of the learned, that I should know how to speak a word in season to him that is weary: He wakeneth morning by morning, He wakeneth mine ear to hear as the learned." Isaiah 50:4.

The Source of Christ's Power

We shall not go far astray if we accept the view that in Christ's prayer, in His communion with the Father, lay His power. When He appeared before the people, He was always calm and composed. The future had been opened to Him; He knew just what He would meet; nothing could come to Him as a surprise, and He was always master of the situation. Nathanael might in surprise ask how He knew him when they had never met before, and Christ quietly answered, "Before that Philip called thee, when thou wast under the fig tree, I saw thee." John 1:48. The woman at the well was so astonished at what He revealed to her that she completely forgot her errand and left her waterpot at the well, while she went into the city and "testified, He told me all that ever I did." John 4:39. All His power, all His composure, all the authority of His words, all the certainty of His statements and predictions, stemmed from His interviews with His Father. His power lay in His prayer, His communion with God.

It is of interest to note that before important events or decisions, Christ spent the preceeding night in the mountains with God. Before His first preaching tour He "departed into a solitary place, and there prayed." Mark 1: 35, 38, 39. Before He chose the twelve disciples "He went out into a mountain to pray, and continued all night in prayer to God. And when it was day, He called unto Him His disciples: and of them He chose twelve, whom also He named apostles." Luke 6:12, 13. At the time of the transfiguration He took Peter and James and John "and went up into the mountain to pray." Luke 9:28. On this occasion "the fashion of His countenance was altered, and His raiment was white and glistering." Verse 29. At the time of His baptism He prayed. Luke 3:21. At the time of the Lord's Supper He prayed; in the garden and on the cross He prayed. Luke 22:19, 41; 23:34. It may safely be said that on every important occasion He prayed, and at times spent the whole night in prayer.

These examples of Christ's prayers demonstrate the possibilities of prayer. Jesus prayed, and even His garments became glistering. How different from our tame and lifeless prayer! Christ prayed until even His garments were affected.

The disciples could not fail to notice that Christ had sources of strength of which they knew nothing. They would work all day long and, when night came, fall asleep exhausted. Christ would forgo sleep, going out to the mountains alone, and when He came back in the morning He was fully refreshed and ready to minister to the people again. The disciples must have wondered where He got such vitality and how He could keep up His work. He said very little if anything of His night vigils, but it must have become clear to them that there was a close connection between His nights of prayer and His days of strength. No wonder they asked Him to teach them to pray.

We have, of course, no record of what took place in those night seasons which Father and Son spent together alone. That it had to do principally with Christ's work seems evident, but beyond this we cannot go. We know that on the mount of transfiguration Moses and Elijah talked "of His decease which He should accomplish at Jerusalem." Luke 9:31. These two men had both been on earth. One had died and been raised again; the other had not tasted death. They were now discussing with Jesus His impending death. They had both been saved and taken to heaven in anticipation of the sacrifice Christ was to make, and truly represented all the saved from all ages, most of whom would taste death, but some of whom would be translated at Christ's coming.

Beyond these few facts we know nothing of those night seasons of prayer. They must have been precious occasions, invigorating to body as well as to soul. Christ did not always have eight hours of sleep. He did not always have regular meals. He had meat of which the disciples did not know; He had sources of strength from above.

The last few days of Christ's ministry on earth He spent instructing His disciples and forwarning them of the events to come. He concluded His instruction with what has come to be called His high-priestly prayer, dedicating them as well as Himself to God. Immediately after the prayer He went to Gethsemane.

This prayer is recorded in the seventeenth chapter of John and contains a résumé of His work. Lifting up His eyes to heaven and addressing His Father, He said, "The hour is come." John 17:1. This was the hour that He had looked forward to with apprehension and He had even thought of asking the Father that He might be saved from it. He immediately rejected such a suggestion, saying that it was for this hour He had come into the world. John 12:27. Would He be able to glorify God in His suffering? Could He calmly face torture and death? This weighed on His mind. For this would be His hour of glory if He victoriously could meet it. All creation was vitally and absorbingly interested in this time when Christ should enter the domain of death and through death wrest from Satan his prey. For Christ this would be the supreme hour, and God would be glorified if He triumphantly passed the test. So He prayed, "Father, glorify Thy name." God answered, "I have both glorified it, and will glorify it again." Verse 28.

The Hour Had Come

Now the hour had come that would decide the world's destiny, and Christ prayed, "Glorify Thy Son, that Thy Son also may glorify Thee." John 17:1. This was a prayer not for glory to the Son as such, but a prayer that God would sustain Him in the ordeal, that when the hour of darkness should come, Christ would be enabled to glorify

God in His death and that through His death Satan
would be defeated. Entering Satan's stronghold to liberate
the prisoners, entering alone to match powers with the
evil one and overcome him and take away from him his
armor, would be a wonderful victory and the deciding
one. Should Christ fail, it would be victory for Satan, and
Christ's work would be in vain. Christ trembled as He
thought of the momentous issues depending upon this
hour, and He said, "Now is My soul troubled." John
12:27. But receiving encouragement that God would sustain and glorify Him, He resolutely exclaimed: "Now is
the judgment of this world: now shall the prince of this
world be cast out." Verse 31.

Christ had so far finished the work given Him to do,
and He now asked God to sustain Him in the dark hour
ahead. John 17:4, 5. He assured the Father, "I have given
unto them the words which Thou gavest Me," and that
they had received them and had believed. Verses 6-8.
Then He prayed, "Holy Father, keep through Thine own
name those whom Thou hast given Me, that they may
be one, as We are." Verse 11.

"While I was with them in the world, I kept them in
Thy name." "I pray not that Thou shouldest take them
out of the world, but that Thou shouldest keep them from
the evil." Verses 12, 15. He prayed that they might be
sanctified, and for their sakes He sanctified Himself; and
then He made the momentous statement, "As Thou hast
sent Me into the world, even so have I also sent them into
the world." Verse 18.

This means nothing less than that as Christ was sent
into the world to reveal the Father, to preach the gospel,
and to heal the sick, so we are sent. His prayer did not
apply to the disciples only, but to them "also which shall
believe on Me through their word." Verse 20. Thus this

prayer reaches to the end of time and takes in every soul
who shall believe. Christ prayed for Peter. "Satan hath
desired to have you," said Christ, "that he may sift you
as wheat: but I have prayed for thee, that thy faith fail
not: and when thou art converted, strengthen thy brethren." Luke 22:31, 32. And now Christ said that He prayed
for all who shall believe on Him "through their word."
John 17:20.

If we take this literally, it means that Christ has prayed
for us, for the reader and for the writer, for all who shall
believe. And for what has He prayed?—"That they all
may be one: . . . that the world may believe that Thou
hast sent Me." Verse 21. The unity of the church is here
mentioned as being effective in helping the world to believe. How important then, that there be no divisions
among God's people, "all one body we." "By this shall
all men know that ye are My disciples, if ye have love one
to another." John 13:35.

"Father, I will." Christ wants His church with Him,
and He makes a definite demand to that end. Then He
closed the prayer with the hope that "the love wherewith
Thou hast loved Me may be in them, and I in them."
John 17:26. Then came Gethsemane.

It will be noted that Christ's prayer is concerned with
others. He planned and prayed for those whom He loved.
He knew what awaited Him. But even in this hour His
thoughts were for others.

23

The Prayers From the Cross

The First Prayer

"Father, forgive them; for they know not what they do." Luke 23:34.

The first word that came from the cross was a prayer of Christ, not for Himself, but for those who were crucifying Him. It was addressed to the Father and asked forgiveness on the ground that "they know not what they do."

Under the circumstances it would be expected that Christ's first prayer would be for Himself and not for others, particularly since at this time they were driving the nails through His hands. But not a murmur is heard, only a prayer; and that for those who were torturing Him! Pain, excruciating, unbearable, racked His body, but calmly He prays, "Father, forgive them." Behold, what love, what compassion!

We accept Christ's statement that they did not know what they were doing; but we have to accept it by faith. They may not have known that they were crucifying "the Prince of life," but they certainly knew that they were taking part in a supreme tragedy, the torturing of an innocent victim of whom Pilate had said that he found no fault in Him. Acts 3:15; Luke 23:4.

Christ's prayer included not only those who were doing the actual crucifying but also those who instigated it, the scribes and Pharisees, and those who bore false testimony against the Lord. But this only makes Christ's prayer the more wonderful. How could Christ pray for such men? How could He find an excuse for them by saying they did not know what they were doing? Only infinite love could do this. We exclaim again, What amazing love, incomprehensible, almost unbelievable!

Christ "carried up our sins in His body to the tree." 1 Peter 2:24 (American Revised Version, margin). This included the sins of weak Pilate, hypocritical Caiaphas, cruel Herod, time-serving Annas; all still had an opportunity for repentance; their cup of iniquity was not yet full. Christ prayed for them; and this He could not have done had the time of their salvation been past. But Christ prayed. And God waited.

A Mighty Incentive

Christ's prayer should be a mighty incentive for the Christian not to give up praying even for such as seem beyond hope. This prayer from the cross gives hope to the vilest sinner, even for such who at the time are reviling and cursing Him.

This prayer holds another lesson for the believing soul. If Christ could pray for such men, are there any conceivable circumstances under which we should not pray for our enemies? They may have spoken ill against us, they may have borne false testimony, they may have reviled and cursed us, they may even have spit upon us and mistreated us, but they have not yet nailed us to a cross. They did all this to Christ. In place of retaliation He prayed for them. He could do no more. "Pray for them which despitefully use you," Christ had said. Matthew 5:44. Christ lived this prayer. So did Stephen. As they stoned him, he "cried with a loud voice, Lord, lay not this sin to their charge. And when he had said this, he fell asleep." Acts 7:60.

"If there be any virtue, and if there be any praise, think on these things." Philippians 4:8. We have been trying to think of some virtue or some good thing in those who crucified Christ. We can excuse those who did the actual nailing, for they were under orders. But we can find nothing good in those who ordered the execution. Christ did. He found enough to justify asking His Father to forgive them. Again we stand amazed at the wonderful God we are serving. He is not willing that *any* should perish. 2 Peter 3:9. Christ praying for those who are crucifying Him! Wonder, ye heavens, and be astonished, O earth! In death agony, forgetful of self, He prays for others, for poor, deluded, evil men.

The Second Prayer

"At the ninth hour Jesus cried with a loud voice, saying, Eloi, Eloi, lama sabachthani? which is, being interpreted, My God, My God, why hast Thou forsaken Me?" Mark 15:34.

This cry was that of an anguished soul in mortal agony. In it we get a deeper insight into the cost of salvation and a greater appreciation of the wonderful plan of redemption. A sudden outburst under tension, a suppressed cry of heart anguish, an involuntary release of pent-up emotion, is a better index of the struggle of a soul than a ream of words. Christ's outcry is an awe-inspiring revelation of the inmost heart of God.

Much has been written on the question of whether the

Father had actually forsaken Christ or Christ merely *thought* He had. This we shall not discuss. In either case Christ's suffering would have been the same.

Christ was to tread the wine press alone, and of the people there was none with Him. See Isaiah 63:3. This was literally fulfilled when all the disciples fled and left Him alone. Mark 14:50. As men had forsaken Him, would God also? His cry clearly indicates that the Father's sustaining presence had been withdrawn.

God's Reaction

The plan of redemption included the death of Christ in the sinner's place. He must feel the wrath of God against sin, die in the place of those who should accept Him, die as the sinner dies, forsaken of God. Moreover, if God is to justify depriving sinners of life, He must by personal experience know the severity of the punishment which He inflicts on His creatures. He must taste of death, and He must also suffer the punishment. The greatest punishment of the sinner is not the final destruction, but the sense of loss that will come to him as he finds himself left out of the kingdom. "There shall be weeping and gnashing of teeth, when ye shall see Abraham, and Isaac, and Jacob, and all the prophets, in the kingdom of God, and you yourselves thrust out." Luke 13:28.

When Christ cried out, "My God, My God, why hast Thou forsaken Me?" it must have wrung the heart of God as He was unable to say, must not say, "Son, I am right here to help You; I have not forsaken You. Be of good courage." But those words must not be spoken. Christ must die alone. Not a ray of light must penetrate the deep darkness. Had He at that time been conscious of the Father's love, had He known that His sacrifice would be accepted and that by His death many would be saved,

He would have been upheld by triumphant joy, and no despairing cry would have escaped Him. But every ray of hope must be removed.

"In yielding up His precious life, Christ was not upheld by triumphant joy. All was oppressive gloom. . . . The wrath of God against sin, the terrible manifestation of His displeasure because of iniquity, filled the soul of His Son with consternation. . . . He cannot see the Father's reconciling face. . . . The Saviour could not see through the portals of the tomb. Hope did not present to Him His coming forth from the grave a conqueror, or tell Him of the Father's acceptance of the sacrifice. He feared that sin was so offensive to God that Their separation was to be eternal. Christ felt the anguish which the sinner will feel when mercy shall no longer plead for the guilty race." —*The Desire of Ages,* pages 752, 753.

There are those who hold that Christ only suffered and not the Father, but this is not supported by Scripture nor by reason. Christ suffered, but the Father no less. To stand by helpless and see the Son spat upon, scourged, reviled, and nailed to the tree must have been supreme torture. No, as the Son suffered, so did the Father. Let no one measure either the suffering or sacrifice of Father and Son and attempt to compare or contrast them. They are beyond human comprehension.

The Third Prayer

"And when Jesus had cried with a loud voice, He said, Father, into Thy hands I commend My spirit: and having said thus, He gave up the ghost." Luke 23:46.

In Gethsemane Jesus said, "Thy will be done." Here He says, "Into Thy hands I commend My spirit." Both statements mean the same. He leaves His case with God.

After Christ's experience in Gethsemane He had been

betrayed, arrested, beaten, scourged, reviled, spat upon, forsaken by all, judged by His own creatures, condemned, and now He was at the point of death, being nailed to the cross. This was what it meant for Him to say, "Thy will be done." He had suffered extreme agony and both physical and spiritual torture. But the worst was the hiding of the Father's face and the blotting out of all hope. What more suffering was in store for Him, He did not know; He could not know. He had drained the dregs of the cup offered Him, and He might be expected to say, "It is enough; I can go no further." But He does not say this. With the last ounce of strength He commits Himself to God, the God who had permitted Him to suffer as no man had ever suffered, with not a murmur of complaint. In committing Himself to God, Christ approves all that has been done and leaves to God His future. He does not for a moment withdraw Himself from what further suffering God may have in store for Him, but confidently commits Himself to God. Then He gives up the ghost and dies. With Job He says, "Though He slay me, yet will I trust in Him." Job 13:15. "Into Thy hands I commend My spirit," is the greatest tribute ever paid God.

Those Three Hours

"And when the sixth hour was come, there was darkness over the whole land until the ninth hour. And at the ninth hour Jesus cried with a loud voice, saying, Eloi, Eloi, lama sabachthani? which is, being interpreted, My God, My God, why hast thou forsaken Me?" Once more Jesus "cried with a loud voice." Mark 15:33, 34, 37. Mark does not tell us what Jesus said at this time, but John informs us that "He said, It is finished: and He bowed His head, and gave up the ghost." John 19:30.

What happened in those last three hours we are not

told. It is clear that it had to do with the new relation between Father and Son as Christ took upon Himself the punishment for the sins of the world, took the sinner's place, and thus exposed Himself to the wrath of God against sin. They were now in the same place where Abraham and Isaac stood as they arrived at the altar and Abraham took the knife to slay his son. Genesis 22. "Abraham rejoiced to see My day," said Christ, "and he saw it, and was glad." John 8:56.

Christ had looked forward with some apprehension to this hour. "Now is My soul troubled," He had said, "and what shall I say? Father, save Me from this hour: but for this cause came I unto this hour." John 12:27. Again He had said, "I have a baptism to be baptized with; and how am I straitened till it be accomplished!" Luke 12:50. This weighed so heavily upon His mind that God had sent two men from heaven to talk the matter over with Him, one who had gone through death, and one who had been translated. Christ had gone up into the mountain to pray, "and as He prayed, the fashion of His countenance was altered, and His raiment was white and glistering. And, behold, there talked with Him two men, which were Moses and Elias: who appeared in glory, and spake of His decease which He should accomplish at Jerusalem." Luke 9:29-31.

We are not told what was said, but we know they "spake of His decease which He should accomplish at Jerusalem." That is, they talked of His death, that which was on His mind and caused Him concern. But in Christ's mind the matter was settled. Should He say, "Father, save Me from this hour"? That could not be; because "for this cause came I unto this hour." John 12:27.

Father and Son had always been close to each other. Says Christ, "I was by Him, as one brought up with

Him: and I was daily His delight, rejoicing always before Him." Proverbs 8:30. He could truthfully say, "He that sent Me is with Me: the Father hath not left Me alone; for I do always those things that please Him." "I and My Father are one." John 8:29; 10:30.

But in the closing hours at the cross Christ could say this no more. The Father was withdrawing Himself. While Christ had been prepared for this, the actual experience was overwhelming. In Gethsemane the preliminary test had come, the test that would demonstrate if Christ could endure the ordeal. There was yet time for Him to turn back. "Christ might even now refuse to drink the cup apportioned to guilty man. It was not yet too late."—*The Desire of Ages,* page 690. At the cross it would be too late.

"Thy will be done." "Three times has He uttered that prayer. Three times has humanity shrunk from the last, crowning sacrifice." But at last His decision is made. "He will save man at any cost to Himself. He accepts His baptism of blood, that through Him perishing millions may gain everlasting life."—*Ibid.,* pp. 690, 693.

Having made this decision, Christ must face the actual test of His ability to endure the reality of the ordeal. "He fell dying to the ground from which He had partially risen. . . . Angels beheld the Saviour's agony. They saw their Lord enclosed by legions of satanic forces, His nature weighed down with a shuddering, mysterious dread. There was silence in heaven. No harp was touched. Could mortals have viewed the amazement of the angelic host as in silent grief they watched the Father separating His beams of light, love, and glory from His beloved Son, they would better understand how offensive in His sight is sin."—*Ibid.,* p. 693.

"In this awful crisis, when everything was at stake,

when the mysterious cup trembled in the hand of the sufferer, the heavens opened." Help was at hand. "The angel came not to take the cup from Christ's hand, but to strengthen Him to drink it, with the assurance of the Father's love. . . . He told Him that He would see of the travail of His soul, and be satisfied."—*Ibid.,* pp. 693, 694.

Christ had stood the test. He had demonstrated that He could come to the point of death and not yield. This was not the final test. That would come at the cross. *Here* He was given the assurance of the Father's love. *There* there would be no such assurance. Concerning those dreadful three hours, this is written: "Amid the awful darkness, apparently forsaken of God, Christ had drained the last dregs in the cup of human woe. In those dreadful hours He had relied upon the evidence of His Father's acceptance heretofore given Him. He was acquainted with the character of His Father; He understood His justice, His mercy, and His great love. By faith He rested in Him whom it had ever been His joy to obey. And as in submission He committed Himself to God, the sense of the loss of His Father's favor was withdrawn. By faith, Christ was victor."—*Ibid.,* p. 756.

24

The Lord's Prayer

MATTHEW and Luke both record the Lord's Prayer. Matthew 6:9-13; Luke 11:2-4. As Matthew's rendering is a little fuller, and the one ordinarily used in worship, we shall use this as the basis of our study. It reads as follows:

"Our Father which art in heaven,
Hallowed be Thy name.
Thy kingdom come.
Thy will be done in earth, as it is in heaven.
Give us this day our daily bread.
And forgive us our debts, as we forgive our debtors.
And lead us not into temptation,
But deliver us from evil:
For Thine is the kingdom, and the power, and the
glory, forever. Amen."

An examination will show that the prayer consists of seven petitions, with an introduction, "Our Father," and the closing doxology, "For Thine is the kingdom." It falls into two main sections. The first section—the first three petitions—is concerned chiefly with the glory of God; the second section—the four latter petitions—is concerned with man's need.

At the time when Christ taught His disciples the Lord's Prayer, He was discussing the manner in which the Pharisees gave alms. They did this in a manner to attract attention to themselves, "that they may have glory of men." Matthew 6:2. They would even sound a trumpet before them to make sure that all would know what they were doing and would give them glory. But this acclaim of men would be all the reward they would get. Said Christ, "They have their reward." Verse 2. He then gave men this advice, "Let not thy left hand know what thy right hand doeth: That thine alms may be in secret: and thy Father which seeth in secret Himself shall reward thee openly." Verses 3, 4.

By a natural transition, He then discussed prayer. This also should be done in secret. "When thou prayest, enter into thy closet, and when thou hast shut thy door, pray to thy Father which is in secret; and thy Father which seeth in secret shall reward thee openly." Verse 6.

Alone in Prayer

During the first thirty years of Christ's life in the crowded house conditions then prevailing it is unlikely that in the home of His parents He had a room of His own where He could retire for prayer. But we are certain that He who taught others to pray in secret found both time and place to be alone with God. When He entered His public work, it was also not easy to be alone. Multitudes followed Him everywhere, and at times there were so many that "they had no leisure so much as to eat." Mark 6:31.

One time when the disciples were tired out with their heavy work of waiting on the multitude, Jesus suggested that they go "into a desert place, and rest awhile." So "they departed into a desert place by ship privately."

In going by boat they hoped the crowd would not follow them. But in this they were disappointed, for when they arrived at the designated place, the people were there already, having gone around the lake by land. Christ, who was also tired, nevertheless "began to teach them many things" (verse 34), miraculously fed the huge multitude, and sent them home. He then "constrained His disciples to get into the ship, and to go to the other side," while He remained behind. Verse 45. He Himself "departed into a mountain to pray." Verse 46.

Alone in a Crowd

At times it was not possible for Christ to get away from the multitude, nor were there always mountains to which He could escape. Under such circumstances He prayed where He was, unconscious of the people around Him and undisturbed by their presence. Note this remarkable statement: "It came to pass, as He was alone praying, His disciples were with Him." Luke 9:18. His disciples were with Him; yet He was alone.

Thus, whatever the conditions were, Christ found a way to be alone with God. In this we do well to follow Him. It may be some quiet place at home; it may be in the workshop or in some dedicated place in the woods or in the garden; it may be even in the barn or the hayloft —any place where the soul can commune alone with his God. If no place can be found, we may have to learn how to be alone with God when others are present. It may be while traveling on plane or on train or ship; it may be while walking on the crowded street or in the field. If we are really intent on having a few words with God we will find opportunity to shut out all other thoughts and commune with Him. There is always time for quiet meditation before we close our eyes in sleep.

God is pleased to have us pray publicly; He is pleased when we are faithful in attending meetings for prayer; He is pleased when we read and study about prayer. But none of these good things must or can take the place of secret prayer. Christ said, "Pray to thy Father which is in secret; and thy Father which seeth in secret shall reward thee openly." Matthew 6:6. This counsel should be heeded. Public prayer, public worship, are commendable and vital. But there is no substitute for the quiet hour with God.

Vain Repetition

"When ye pray, use not vain repetitions, as the heathen do: for they think that they shall be heard for their much speaking. Be not ye therefore like unto them: for your Father knoweth what things ye have need of, before ye ask Him." Verses 7, 8.

"Your Father knoweth." He knows what we ask, and He knows what we need. The two are not always the same. He has promised to supply our needs, but not necessarily our wants. There are times when we ask for things which we would like to have, when a little planning would show that we do not need them as much as we sometimes think we do. God knows this; and hence God may think it best not to give us what we want.

Prayer is not primarily designed to get us things; it is rather to teach us to be content with such things as we have. Paul said, "Be content with such things as ye have." Hebrews 13:5. "Having food and raiment let us be therewith content." 1 Timothy 6:8. "Godliness with contentment is great gain." Verse 6. Paul lived up to his preaching. He said, "I have learned, in whatsoever state I am, therewith to be content." Philippians 4:11.

This does not mean that we are not to strive for something better, to improve our lot. Nor does it mean that we are to be content with ourselves and our progress mentally or spiritually. We are ever to strive for a higher goal as far as we are concerned. We are to be content with what we *have,* but not with what we *are.* Too often the reverse is the case: We are content with what we are, discontented with what we have. The following advice is to the point:

> Could'st thou in vision see thyself the man God meant,
> Thou never more could'st be the man thou art, content.

Could we but have a vision of what God meant us to be we would never be content with what we are. "Higher than the highest human thought can reach is God's ideal for His children."

A Besetting Sin

Discontent is one of the besetting sins of the age, and it is not one to which worldlings only are subject. There are too many discontented Christians, too many disgruntled church members, too many covetous, dissatisfied saints. In our looks and attitudes we do not always give men a correct picture of the joys of Christianity. With our lips we praise God, but our looks are telling the world that God is not a good Master. If in a home the mother is always downcast and discouraged, the children dissatisfied and sullen, we might rightly draw the conclusion that things are not right in that home, and that probably both father and mother are lacking in certain vital aspects. This is also the conclusion one has a right to draw when God's children murmur and complain. We are giving God a bad reputation when we fail to show in our lives the joyfulness of serving the Lord.

"After this manner therefore pray ye." Matthew 6:9. "Therefore" has reference to the advice Christ has just given, that we are not to display our prayers by standing praying in the synagogues or in the street corners to be seen of men, but that we are to pray in secret, avoiding vain repetitions. To help us form our petitions, to teach us to pray, He now gives us a sample prayer. We do not understand that this is the only prayer we are to use. We may still pour out our souls to God; we may still pray from the heart as God gives us utterance. But the Lord's Prayer teaches us what is to be included in our prayers, and it does this without the use of vain repetitions. It does not use many words, but is comprehensive, all-inclusive. It is a Christ-ordained prayer, and should have a place in our worship. It fits the individual soul; it fits the family; it fits the church. Even little children can early learn to join the other members of the household in its simple wording.

"Our Father"

"Our Father." Christians are here taught to say "Our Father," not "My Father." This opening statement makes the prayer a true, universal Christian prayer in that it recognizes the Fatherhood of God and the brotherhood of man. "Mine house," said the prophet, "shall be called an house of prayer for all people." Isaiah 56:7. Christ endorsed this when He said, "Is it not written, My house shall be called of all nations the house of prayer?" Mark 11:17.

If men of every nation may address God as Father, then all men are brethren, whether they are white, black, brown, red, or yellow. "All ye are brethren." Matthew 23:8. Among non-Christians it may be expected that some people should consider themselves better than others, and one nation superior to its neighbor. "But it shall not be so among you," said Christ, "but whosoever will be great among you, let him be your minister; and whosoever will be chief among you, let him be your servant." Matthew 20:26, 27.

No Christian can honestly repeat this first phrase of the Lord's Prayer and consider himself superior to others. God is not the Father of the Europeans only, or of Americans, or of Australians. He is the Father of all. There is no respecter of persons with God; neither should there be among Christians.

"Father," which in the original Greek and in many translations is the first word in the prayer, is the endearing term which Jesus used in addressing the First Person of the Godhead, and which He permits us to use.

The idea of the universal Fatherhood of God has been of slow acceptance because of the necessary corollary of the universal brotherhood of men. Says the prophet, "Have we not all one Father? hath not one God created us?" Malachi 2:10. In God's sight there is no master race nor any slave race. One man was not created to ride, another to be ridden. Let those who use and revere the Lord's Prayer have this in mind. The prayer begins with a declaration of the Fatherhood of God, and hence of the unity, dignity, and high origin of all men. "All ye are brethren."

In permitting us to call God our Father, Christ considers all men as belonging to the family of God, with all the honors, responsibilities, and privileges devolving upon children of such high rank. All should walk worthy of the calling wherewith they are called.

To an Indian, God is an Indian; to a Chinese, He is a Chinese; to an American, He is an American. Each nation thinks of God as having its own peculiar national characteristics and physiognomy. But God is not a national God; He is not partial to any race, white, black, or brown. He is the God of all; He is the Father of all. This may be disappointing to some who would like to have God in their own image. "Of course God is an American," said a young lady to me. "What else could He be?"

It would be better if artists ceased to make images or pictures of God. "No man hath seen God at any time." John 1:18. How, then, can anyone make a picture of Him? It is just as unreasonable as attempting to make a picture of the Holy Spirit. Such would be blasphemy. And so is making images of God.

"Father" stands for love, protection, companionship, understanding, guidance, correction, watchcare, compassion. God possesses all these attributes, and doubtless many others, and, being our Father and the cause of our existence, has the strongest reasons for exercising His powers in our behalf. We are not to come to Him as to a stranger, or even primarily as to a God, but as to a Father who is bound to us with bands of love, cords that will ever hold. To Him we can open our hearts. In Him we can safely trust.

"Which Art in Heaven"

We are wont to think of heaven as being above us, and rightly so. To look up to heaven is to look up to God's dwelling place. But when those who live on the other side of the earth look up, they look in the exact opposite direction from what we do; and, lo, there is God also. From whatever point on earth we look to heaven, there is God, surrounding and enclosing us and the whole earth. "If I ascend up into heaven, Thou art there: if I make my bed in hell, behold, Thou art there. If I take the wings of the morning, and dwell in the uttermost parts of the sea; even there shall Thy hand lead me, and Thy right hand shall hold me." Psalm 139:8-10. No place on earth is nearer to heaven than is any other place. God is everywhere, and wherever I go, God is there to guide and uphold me.

In some respects the Father is the forgotten person of the Godhead. In innumerable sermons Christ is exalted and His name constantly mentioned, as it should be. In word and song the Spirit is magnified, as is right and proper. But seldom do we hear a sermon of which the Father is the subject. We are in danger of forgetting the Father of all, or relegating Him to a secondary place.

There is no jealousy in the heavenly Trio. The Father is pleased to hear praise given to the Son and the Holy Spirit. But we think it well not to ignore the Father in our devotions, sermons, and hymns of praise. Christ devoted much time to inform His disciples of the Father. We will do well to study Christ's teaching on this subject.

One of the reasons Christ came to this earth was to reveal the Father to men. The world knew but little of God, and practically all had a wrong conception of Him. To set men right, to give them a true view of the character of God, Christ became man. He was God "manifest in the flesh." 1 Timothy 3:16. Men looked upon Him, and as they did they saw the Father. John 14:9.

Not only did the world not know God; His own people, the Jews, did not know Him. They thought of Him as creator, judge, and lawgiver, but not as a kind and understanding Father. This was largely the fault of their leaders. In the time of Christ it was especially the fault of the Pharisees. They gave the impression that God had not made the Sabbath for man, but man for the Sabbath. No true Jew would minister to the sick on the Sabbath; that would be sacrilege. To carry to a sick person a glass of water would be carrying a burden on the Sabbath and

was forbidden. The commandment "Thou shalt not kill"
was interpreted to include insects, and hence some holy
persons would carry with them a small broom with which
to sweep before them, lest they step on a worm or insect
and thus be guilty of murder. Some would hold a cloth
before their eyes lest they look on evil and be guilty, and
others would do equally irrational things. From such conduct the people gained a wrong idea of the Father. They
saw Him not as a loving and compassionate Father, but
as an unreasonable and harsh God, an unjust judge, who
delighted in making rules impossible to keep and who
would punish those who disobeyed.

Christ's teaching about God was directly opposed to
that of the Pharisees. In healing the sick, comforting the
mourners, raising the dead, and forgiving sins He was
giving men a picture of what God is like. Said He, "He
that hath seen Me hath seen the Father." John 14:9. "I
and My Father are one." John 10:30. Men were charmed
by His gracious words, as well as mightily moved by
them. As He went about spreading good cheer, attending
a wedding feast when He thought best, accepting invita-
tions to eat with people, always kind and considerate to
all, men could not fail to see the vivid contrast between
His practice and the teaching of the Pharisees. Christ was
revealing God to men.

A true doctrine of God is of vital concern to all. If a
wrong doctrine can produce the Inquisition, we must not
think lightly of studying carefully "the doctrine of God
our Saviour." Titus 2:10. For "he that abideth in the doctrine of Christ, he hath both the Father and the Son."
2 John 9. John considered this so important that he declared, "If there come any unto you, and bring not this
doctrine, receive him not into your house, neither bid him
Godspeed." Verse 10.

When we pray, "Our Father," we invoke the help of One who is truly our Father, who loves and cares for us, and will do anything to help us. He will guide us, counsel us, correct us if need be; but He will do it in love. May we ever keep sacred His name, the name of Father.

"Hallowed Be Thy Name"

"Hallowed be Thy name" is the first of the seven petitions in the Lord's Prayer. It concerns the reverence due His holy name. As God Himself is holy, so is His name. We pray that we may hallow that holy name, hold it in reverence.

In Old Testament times a name generally mirrored some outstanding characteristic in the person named. Thus Jacob earned his name because of the unreliability of his character. Genesis 27:36. He had difficulty telling the truth. After his experience with the angel (Genesis 32:28), God changed his name from Jacob, a deceiver, to Israel, an overcomer.

Mary, the mother of Jesus, before the birth of her son was commanded, "Thou shalt call His name Jesus: for He shall save His people from their sins." Matthew 1:21. Jesus, Saviour, was to be His name, for He should save His people.

If God's name is to signify all that He is, it must be a special name. And it is. God Himself chose it as the summation of all His attributes, an expression of His total being and eternal existence, the Almighty, the One "which is, and which was, and which is to come." Revelation 1:4.

Moses had been chosen by God as leader of Israel. As such it would be his work to go to Egypt, where Israel was in bondage, and persuade the king to let them go. He was also to gather Israel together and persuade them to go. Both of these missions were hard ones, and Moses hesitated to accept this work. He was unknown to the Israelites, having left Egypt forty years before, and he knew it would be a herculean task to persuade a whole nation to leave all their property and start on a journey that would bring them into a barren desert. He felt that he must have divine credentials, or he could never succeed. So he said to God, "When I come unto the children of Israel, and shall say unto them, The God of your fathers hath sent me unto you; and they shall say to me, What is His name? what shall I say unto them? And God said unto Moses, I AM THAT I AM: and He said, Thus shalt thou say unto the children of Israel, I AM hath sent me unto you." Exodus 3:13, 14. In the next verse God explains further. "Thus shalt thou say unto the children of Israel, The Lord God of your fathers, the God of Abraham, the God of Isaac, and the God of Jacob, hath sent me unto you: this is My name forever, and this is My memorial unto all generations." Verse 15.

This is indeed a strange name; but it is the name God Himself chose. It is His name forever, and His memorial unto all generations. It denotes the Ever-living One, the Self-existing One, the One who always has been and always will be. The original Hebrew word is JHVH,— Hebrew was originally written without vowel sounds,— and this name was probably pronounced YAHWEH, from which we get the word Jehovah. The word YAHWEH occurs thousands of times in the Old Testament, and in the American Revised Version is always translated Jehovah, while the King James Version translates it LORD GOD, written in small capitals. When the reader finds LORD GOD in his Authorized Version, he may know that the original is *Jehovah,* God's self-chosen name, the I AM.

This name was counted so sacred by the Jews that it was never pronounced by them. Not only did they not pronounce it, they were even forbidden to think it. When they came to it in their reading, publicly or privately, they substituted in its stead ADONAI.

The name *Jehovah* becomes of interest to us as we learn that commentators in general hold that *Jehovah* in the King James Version is the name of the Second Person of the Godhead, Christ. The I AM who told Moses that this was His name forever, is the same who calmly told the Jews that He was the I AM. John 8:58. "It was Christ who from the bush on Mount Horeb spoke to Moses saying, 'I AM THAT I AM.'"—*The Desire of Ages,* page 24. When Christ with solemn dignity told the Jews, "Verily, verily, I say unto you, Before Abraham was, I AM," "silence fell upon the vast assembly. The name of God, given to Moses to express the idea of the eternal presence, had been claimed as His own by this Galilean Rabbi. He had announced Himself to be the Self-existent One, He who had been promised to Israel, 'whose goings forth have been from of old, from the days of eternity.'" —*Ibid.,* pp. 469, 470. "Then took they up stones to cast at Him." John 8:59.

This was not the only time that Christ claimed to be the I AM. One time when the disciples saw Christ walking on the water, they cried out in fear, thinking they saw a spirit. Mark 6:47-50. Christ calmed them by saying, "Be of good cheer: it is I; be not afraid." Verse 50. The Greek reads, "Be of good cheer. I AM." "And the wind ceased." Verse 51.

The name I AM stands for the revealed character of God. This is made clear in God's answer to Moses' request that he be shown His glory. Exodus 33:18. Said God, "I will make all My goodness pass before thee, and I will proclaim the name of the Lord before thee." Verse 19.

Accordingly, "the Lord descended in the cloud, and stood with him there, and proclaimed the name of the Lord. And the Lord passed by before him, and proclaimed, The Lord, The Lord God, merciful and gracious, long-suffering, and abundant in goodness and truth, keeping mercy for thousands, forgiving iniquity and transgression and sin, and that will by no means clear the guilty; visiting the iniquity of the fathers upon the children, and upon the children's children, unto the third and to the fourth generation." Exodus 34:5-7.

The Lord did not proclaim to Moses a name as such. He let His "goodness" pass before him, and *that* was His name. He told Moses what He *was,* naming His attributes, His character, His inmost self, His complete personality. *That* is His name. In effect God said, What I AM, that is My name. And this He summed up in the Hebrew word YAHWEH, or Jehovah, I AM THAT I AM, or as some translate, I AM WHAT I AM. What God is, that is His name.

Christ is the great I AM, that "ever liveth," "the Prince of life," "Spirit of life." Hebrews 7:25; Acts 3:15; Romans 8:2. With Him there "is no variableness, neither shadow of turning." James 1:17. He is "the same yesterday, and today, and forever." Hebrews 13:8. That is why His name is I AM. When we think of the past, of the days of Abraham, there is the I AM; or if we think of the future, the "forever," there is the I AM also. He ever liveth.

For another reason than that mentioned above, the name of God becomes of special interest to the church of God today; for as John looked, "lo, on Mount Zion stood the Lamb, and with Him a hundred and forty-four thousand who had His name and His Father's name written on their foreheads." Revelation 14:1, R.S.V. This means that they had the character of God impressed upon them.

This name is that which was revealed to Moses when God came down on Mount Sinai and let His goodness pass before him and proclaimed the name of the Lord. Exodus 34:4-7. In view of this it may be profitable to look a little more closely at the attributes listed, for, as far as these attributes are applicable to mankind, the 144,000 will possess them. This is a high honor and a high responsibility.

In this first petition of the Lord's Prayer we express our desire to keep holy and sacred the name of God. Strange that this name should be the one which the world most misuses and takes in vain! God's name is dragged in the filth and slime of obscene curses and oaths and is coupled with Satan's name in blasphemy. We cannot at all times shut ourselves out of hearing this, but we can be warned not to get so accustomed to hearing foul language that it ceases to shock us.

As we are commanded to keep holy the Sabbath day, so we are admonished to hallow God's name, for "holy and reverend is His name." Psalm 111:9. When we become Christians we are adopted as members of the family of God and take His name upon us. This name we are not to take in vain; we are not to profane it or bring it in ill repute. Most families are jealous of their reputation and their good name, and guard it carefully from becoming identified with anything that is questionable. God also is jealous of His name and His family.

We must not lower the standard which God has set for His people and which He has made possible of attainment by the abundant provision He has made for man to live above sin. But we wish to encourage those who find themselves coming short of their intentions, or who have been taught that the goal is unattainable. Let such be of good cheer. "A just man falleth seven times, and riseth up again." Proverbs 24:16. "The steps of a good man are ordered by the Lord: and he delighteth in His way. Though he fall, he shall not be utterly cast down: for the Lord upholdeth him with His hand." Psalm 37:23, 24. "Rejoice not against me, O mine enemy: when I fall, I shall arise; when I sit in darkness, the Lord shall be a light unto me." Micah 7:8.

God reckons as perfect those who may yet be far from the end of the race, but whose heart is perfect toward Him, who are on the right road and facing in the right direction. They are struggling on, but appear to make little progress. God looks in pity upon them, and though they fall seven times, He will lift them up and cheer them on. It is not necessarily how far a man has come that counts. It is the direction in which he is going that matters.

Hear these heartening words: "When it is in the heart to obey God, when efforts are put forth to this end, Jesus accepts this disposition and effort as man's best service, and He makes up for the deficiency with His own divine merits."—Ellen G. White, *Signs of the Times,* June 16, 1890.

God admonishes His people to be holy. Leviticus 19:2. He told Abraham to be perfect. Genesis 17:1. He calls Noah perfect. Genesis 6:9. It is evident that the perfection or holiness which these men had or strove for was not the final perfection of God or of the saints in glory.

It is possible for a thing or a person to be perfect and yet not perfected. "The bud is perfect," says Isaiah. Isaiah 18:5. So is the seed, the newborn lamb, the acorn. These things are perfect in every state of development, but full perfection awaits the time of ripening. An apple from the time of the first bloom may be perfect though it is yet green and unfit for food. When at last it is ripe, it is perfected.

Paul informed us that he had not "already attained, either were already perfect." Philippians 3:12. He had not reached the goal he had set for himself. But "I press toward the mark," he said. Verse 14. Then, having in mind those who with him were pressing forward, he said, "Let *us* therefore, as many as *be perfect,* be thus minded." Verse 15. In verse 15, by the use of the word "us," he included himself in those who claim perfection.

In these verses Paul exemplified the Biblical use of the word perfect. God counts those perfect who press on and are "thus minded." "If there be first a willing mind, it is accepted according to that a man hath, and not according to that he hath not." 2 Corinthians 8:12. According to this principle we are admonished to go on "perfecting holiness in the fear of God." 2 Corinthians 7:1. The man who is on the right road will at last be counted as having attained, even though he was yet far from perfection.

The prayer "Hallowed be Thy name" is a prayer of consecration, a prayer for purity and holiness. It is the first petition in the Lord's Prayer and thus gives holiness its rightful place. It calls upon men to dedicate themselves to God, to be jealous of His holy name as they become members of the family of God.

"Thy Kingdom Come"

The kingdom of God for which we are to pray includes three distinct ideas:

1. The kingdom of God on earth, His visible church, consisting of those who have willingly enlisted under His banner. Exodus 19:6; 1 Peter 2:9.

2. The kingdom of God "within you," the invisible kingdom, consisting of all honest believers anywhere, without regard to church affiliation. Luke 17: 21.

3. The kingdom of heaven, when "the kingdoms of

this world are become the kingdoms of our Lord, and of His Christ." Matthew 8:11; 2 Timothy 4:18; Revelation 11:15.

Christ's preaching concerned itself almost entirely with the "gospel of the kingdom," which might mean any one of the three named, or all three, as the context indicates.

In the beginning of His ministry, Christ "came into Galilee, preaching the gospel of the kingdom of God, and saying, The time is fulfilled, and the kingdom of God is at hand: repent ye, and believe the gospel." Mark 1:14, 15. "Jesus went about all the cities and villages, teaching in their synagogues, and preaching the gospel of the kingdom." Matthew 9:35; 4:23. When the people in a certain place asked Him to stay with them, He declined to do so, saying, "I must preach the kingdom of God to other cities also." Luke 4:42, 43.

The disciples followed the lead of their Master. When He sent out the Twelve He commanded them "to preach the kingdom of God, and to heal the sick." Luke 9:2. When He sent out the seventy, they received this commission: "Say unto them, The kingdom of God is come nigh unto you." Luke 10:9. It is of note that when Christ said that the gospel is to be preached in all the world for a witness to all nations, He designated it as *"this* gospel of the kingdom." Matthew 24:14. Christ considered the gospel of the kingdom so important that He put it first on the list of that for which men shall seek. Said He, "Seek ye first the kingdom of God, and His righteousness; and all these things shall be added unto you." Matthew 6:31-33.

When Pilate asked Christ, "Art Thou the King of the Jews?" He answered, "My kingdom is not of this world." John 18:33, 36. When Pilate pressed Him further, "Art Thou a king then? Jesus answered, Thou sayest that I am a king," an affirmative reply. Christ *was* a king, but His kingdom was not of this world.

In the beginning God created the heavens and the earth. "The heaven, even the heavens, are the Lord's," says David, "but the earth hath He given to the children of men." Psalm 115:16. When the earth was given to Adam, he became, under God, its ruler. When man sinned and came under the dominion of sin, Satan promptly claimed the earth as his and felt emboldened to offer it to Christ on condition of submission and worship. Showing Christ "all the kingdoms of the world, and the glory of them," Satan said, "All these things will I give Thee, if Thou wilt fall down and worship me." Matthew 4:8, 9. Satan had assumed charge of this earth, had become its prince, and taken men captive. Christ had come to wrest this dominion from Satan, liberate the prisoners, and establish His own kingdom. Satan understood this, and his first plan was to win over Christ and, if this failed, to tempt and torture Him in an effort to discourage Him from finishing His work. Unless in some way he could overcome Christ he knew that his own doom was sealed.

Christ also knew what was at stake. If He failed, all would be lost. Satan would then have undisputed control, and this world would be his kingdom. Once before, Satan had claimed control over the earth when, as a self-appointed representative from this world, he met with the sons of God as recorded in the book of Job. When God pointed to Job as the true representative, Satan sneeringly answered, "Doth Job fear God for nought? . . . Put forth Thine hand now, and touch all that he hath, and he will curse Thee to Thy face." Job 1:9-11. In the test that ensued, Job won, and Satan retired defeated.

Once more Satan tried it, and again he was defeated. After this he appears no more in the book. Job stood the test. Satan was not God's representative. Job was.

From any human viewpoint Christ's task was impossible. Having taken on the nature of man, how could He ever expect to cope with the powers of darkness? His plan was to win men from the army of Satan, deliver them from the power of darkness, and translate them into the kingdom of heaven. See Colossians 1:13. This would necessitate that Christ attack the stronghold of Satan, who as a "strong man fully armed guardeth his own court." Luke 11:21, R.V.

If Christ was "to bring out the prisoners from the prison, and them that sit in darkness out of the prison house" (Isaiah 42:7), He would have to enter the prison house Himself and become subject to death; but having in His possession the keys of hell and of death (Revelation 1:18), He would open the prison door, walk out, and take with Him those who wished to be liberated.

This is the very thing He did. At the time of His death "the graves were opened; and many bodies of the saints which slept arose, and came out of the graves after His resurrection, and went into the Holy City, and appeared unto many." Matthew 27:52, 53. Thus it was possible for Christ through death to "destroy him that had the power of death, that is, the devil; and deliver them who through fear of death were all their lifetime subject to bondage." Hebrews 2:14, 15.

As stated above, it was Satan's plan to get Christ to sin, if that were possible, for He would thus come under Satan's control. Satan did his best in the temptation in the wilderness, but did not succeed. He did his best all through the time of the ministry of Christ, but again he failed. He tried it again in Gethsemane, but found no foothold whatsoever. Said Christ, "The prince of this world cometh, and hath nothing in Me." John 14:30.

Christ repelled every dart thrown at Him, resisted every temptation. Successfully He challenged the Jews, "Which of you convinceth Me of sin?" and there was no answer. John 8:46.

As the climax in the life of Christ approached, the time which Jesus called "your hour, and the power of darkness," (Luke 22:53), when He, singlehanded and alone, should enter the domain of death and wrest from Satan "the captives of the mighty" (Isaiah 49:25), His humanity shrank from the magnitude and apparent impossibility of the task. John gives us a glimpse of the inner struggle of Jesus when he quoted Him as saying, "Now is My soul troubled; and what shall I say? Father, save Me from this hour: but for this cause came I unto this hour." John 12:27.

These are pathetic words as coming from the Saviour. The hour had come, and His human nature quailed before the horror of torture and death. A call to His Father for help would bring Him more than twelve legions of angels. Matthew 26:53. But was it not for this very purpose that He had come to the world? No, He could not ask to be saved from the agonizing test. But the very fact that He thought of it, reveals His humanity.

Only for a moment did Christ hesitate. Resolutely His faith asserted itself. He would go forward. He would glorify God. And souls would be saved. He looked to heaven and said, "Father, glorify Thy name. Then came there a voice from heaven, saying, I have both glorified it, and will glorify it again." John 12:28. God had glorified Him in His work on earth, which was to culminate in His death, and would glorify Him again in raising Him from the dead.

Christ's decision was made. He would willingly fulfill His part of the covenant made in heaven. God would not fail Him, but stand by Him. He had just received confirmation that God had glorified and would glorify Him. The prophet of old had asked the question, "Shall the prey be taken from the mighty, or the lawful captive delivered?" Isaiah 49:24. And the answer had come: "The captives of the mighty *shall* be taken away, and the prey of the terrible *shall* be delivered." Verse 25. God's promise was sure: "The Lord God will help me; therefore shall I not be confounded: therefore have I set my face like a flint, and I know that I shall not be ashamed." Isaiah 50:7. With these promises in mind, Christ confidently announced, "Now shall the prince of this world be cast out." John 12:31.

When Christ said this, He knew what the cost would be. He would have to enter the prison house of death. But He was ready. He had the keys that would free Him and the captives.

Some think that it was no struggle for Christ to engage Satan in battle, even to the death. Did not Christ know that He would come out victorious? Had He not in heaven measured the cost? Why was not all, then, clear?

We have mentioned before that in heaven He and the Father had counted every step and knew the cost. But it was necessary for Christ to go over the ground again and as *man* decide what He would do. Even if He were willing to go on with the plan, was He assured of success? Could human nature endure the trial? Should He ask the Father to spare Him from the approaching hour? The fact that He mentioned it at all, reveals His inner struggle. He need not have revealed to man that there was any struggle at all. When He does reveal it, He does it for the purpose of giving us an insight into the deepest recesses of His mind, that we might understand that the cost made Him tremble, that He knew the tremendous battle He must wage, and that in full knowledge of the cost He made His decision. Let no one think that Christ was not tempted.

The prayer, "Thy kingdom come," has been called a glorious prayer of infinite scope. The Jews were much interested in the coming of the kingdom and incorporated petitions for its coming into their common prayers. Some of the rabbis held that any prayer that did not mention the kingdom was no prayer at all.

For the Christian this prayer for the kingdom is of the deepest significance, particularly for those living at this time in the history of this world. The prayer for the establishment of the kingdom of God embraces the incarnation of Christ and His life in humanity, the temptation in the wilderness, Gethsemane and Golgotha, the resurrection and judgment, the destruction of Satan and his kingdom, and the new creation. It is a prayer that God's plan of salvation may come to fruition, that there might be an end of sin, and that righteousness might reign.

The prayer also contemplates the preparation of the saints for participation in the kingdom to come. In coming to this world Christ did His part of the work in destroying the power of the devil. He is now preparing a place for His redeemed in the world to come. But He left a work for us to do in preparing men for citizenship in the new kingdom. He will help us in this, but we have a definite responsibility and important decisions to make. No one can do this for us.

On one occasion the Pharisees asked Christ when the kingdom of God should come. Luke 17:20. The question was probably prompted by the fact that while Jesus preached much about the kingdom, He made no practical provision for its organization. The first requirements would be a reasonably large following and the selection of a few capable men of experience to compose the nucleus of the governing body. Christ had none of these. The few that followed Him were of the common people, and the disciples were unlearned, inexperienced men. No kingdom could ever be established on such a foundation. In contempt the Pharisees had asked, "Have any of the rulers or of the Pharisees believed on Him?" John 7:48. They were certain that Christ could not establish a kingdom without them, but thus far He had not made any approach to them or asked them for help. Evidently they were to be left out. So, to confuse Him they asked when the kingdom should come. Christ "answered them and said, The kingdom of God cometh not with observation: neither shall they say, Lo here! or, lo there! for, behold, the kingdom of God is within you." Luke 17:20, 21.

Christ here emphasized the truth that numbers alone are not a safe criterion of success. Mohammed quickly recruited millions of followers. So did Buddha, and so have apostate churches. The time will come when all the world will wonder after the beast. See Revelation 13:3. Numbers are no evidence of success. In contrast with this, Christ spoke of His church as the little flock. "Fear not, little flock," He said, "for it is your Father's good pleasure to give you the kingdom." Luke 12:32.

It is not safe to count outward prosperity as a sign of God's approval or blessing. We rightly rejoice when we see God's cause prosper and read of the many accessions to the church. But God is not impressed by statistics. We should be careful lest we number Israel and prove by means of arithmetic that God is with us. "There is no restraint to the Lord to save by many or by few." 1 Samuel 14:6. If Christ were on earth now and His work were evaluated by the converts He had at the time of His death, some question might be raised about His success.

Figures measure outward growth, but God looks to the heart. The visible church can be numbered, but the figures do not correspond with the books of heaven. There are many on the church roll that God does not include in His church, and there are many that God includes whose names are not on our books. But it will not always be thus. Said Christ, "Other sheep I have, which are not of this fold: them also I must bring, and they shall hear My voice; and there shall be one fold, and one shepherd." John 10:16. At that time the books in heaven and the books on earth will agree. Happy day! We shall see eternal values as God sees them.

"The kingdom of God is within you." "The Lord seeth not as man seeth; for man looketh on the outward appearance, but the Lord looketh on the heart." 1 Samuel 16:7. It is not numbers, riches, fame, learning, or worldly attainments that interest God. "Heaven is My throne, and the earth is My footstool," said He. Isaiah 66:1. Material things do not count with God, "for all those things hath Mine hand made." Verse 2. He then raised the question, "Where is the place of My rest?" and answered it: "To this man will I look, even to him that is poor and of a contrite spirit, and trembleth at My word." Verses 1, 2. God inhabits eternity; He dwells "in the high and holy place, with him also that is of a contrite and humble spirit." Isaiah 57:15.

Christ's Longings

From these statements we gather that material things do not impress God, "for all those things hath Mine hand made." He made the heavens with all their glory and beauty, and He inhabits eternity. Yet He longs for something which man only can supply—the love of a pure, redeemed soul.

14—P

Christ felt this longing while on earth. "The loneliness of Christ, separated from the heavenly courts, living the life of humanity, was never understood or appreciated by the disciples as it should have been. He was often grieved because His disciples did not give Him that which He should have received from them."—*The Desire of Ages,* page 565. A vivid illustration of Christ's hunger for the love of man is revealed in the question He asked Peter, repeated three times: "Simon, son of Jonas, lovest thou Me?" John 21:17. This was after the resurrection. Christ could have gone to heaven and there received the worship and adoration of the heavenly host. This would have been wonderful, but not enough. "He longed for human tenderness, courtesy, and affection."—*The Desire of Ages,* page 524. This the angels could not give, for they had not been permitted to follow Him in His humiliation. Hear these wonderful words: "If a man love Me, he will keep My words: and My Father will love him, and We will come unto him, and make Our abode with him." John 14:23. And to the last church Christ said, "Behold, I stand at the door, and knock: if any man hear My voice, and open the door, I will come in to him, and will sup with him, and he with Me." Revelation 3:20. Let us open the door.

The prayer that the kingdom come will not be fully answered until we reach the earth made new. This prayer brings to us the responsibility to do all in our power to help bring about its fulfillment. We have a definite work to do, for the gospel of the kingdom must be preached in all the world before the end can come. These two things, therefore, we must do: preach the gospel, and prepare ourselves for that great event. It is of little use that we pray for the kingdom to come, if we do nothing to further its coming. As we begin to comprehend more fully the meaning of this prayer we agree with the statement that no prayer is real prayer that does not include the kingdom.

It is a serious question how far a Christian can honestly pray for the kingdom to come, while making every preparation to stay in this world. We know that Christ said in the parable, "Occupy till I come." Luke 19:13. This has been made to mean that we may build and carry on as usual, when the word has no such meaning. In the parable of the nobleman "he called his ten servants, and delivered them ten pounds, and said unto them, Occupy till I come." The Revised Version says, "Trade ye herewith till I come." That is, "Use the talents I have given you." The Greek means "to be busy with, to trade." The servants had been given ten talents. Now the nobleman said, Trade with them; get busy. That this is the meaning is evident from the parable itself, for when the master returned, he called the servants together "that he might know how much every man had gained by trading." To apply this parable to anything else than trading with the talents each man had received, is to wrest Scripture.

This, then, is our work while we are waiting for the Lord to come. Busily engaged in the work of God, we may justify our existence. Let us trade with the one talent we have, and God may give us another.

"Thy Will Be Done"

"Thy will be done in earth, as it is in heaven." This petition is built on the fact that God's will is not now being done in earth. If God's will were done, there would be no war or hatred among nations. There would be no injustice or cruelty, no sickness, sorrow, suffering, or tears. Peace and prosperity would prevail, joy and happiness reign supreme.

How have present conditions come about? They are

the results of the selfishness, ambition, and greed of men who have forgotten that they are their brother's keeper. As a consequence some nations have an abundance of that for which others are starving. There is enough food in the world for all, but men have not learned the blessing of sharing with those who are less fortunate. Men have forgotten the golden rule; they have forgotten God.

God's will is well expressed by the prophet who said, "I know the thoughts that I think toward you, saith the Lord, thoughts of peace, and not of evil, to give you an expected end." Jeremiah 29:11. The Revised Standard Version more correctly reads, "I know the plans I have for you, says the Lord, plans for welfare and not for evil, to give you a future and a hope." When this was written, Israel had sinned grievously, and it appeared that there was no future for them. But God had plans for them and encouraged them to try once more. He promised that if they would search for Him with all their heart, He would hear them and would turn their captivity. Jeremiah 39: 12-14.

God is not an angry God who lies in wait to catch men off their guard so He can punish them. Hear these heartening promises: God "doth not afflict willingly nor grieve the children of men." Lamentations 3:33. If God at times must punish, He does it reluctantly. He is "not willing that any should perish, but that all should come to repentance." 2 Peter 3:9. His desire is to "have all men to be saved, and to come unto the knowledge of the truth." 1 Timothy 2:4. From the very beginning God has "chosen you to salvation through sanctification of the Spirit and belief of the truth." 2 Thessalonians 2:13. "This is the will of God, even your sanctification." 1 Thessalonians 4:3.

These texts reveal God's plan for men, all men. He wants every man saved, and is not willing that even one should be lost. His plan includes both a hope and a future, on the condition that we seek Him with all our heart.

When we therefore pray that God's will be done in earth as it is in heaven we align ourselves with divine power to bring this about. Just what, specifically, does God want us to do so that He can work out His plan in us? What is my duty?

A government expresses its will through its laws. Each nation ordinarily has a fundamental law, written or unwritten, generally called "a constitution," which is binding upon all the people. This constitution prescribes and defines the duties of the citizens and is the standard to which all other laws must conform. In a country ruled by a dictator there is no constitution. The will of the dictator is the supreme law, from which there is no appeal.

When God formed Israel into a nation, He publicly entered into a covenant with the people, upon adherence to which they were to become His people and receive His blessings. Moses thus records the event: "And ye came near and stood under the mountain; and the mountain burned with fire unto the midst of heaven, with darkness, clouds, and thick darkness. And the Lord spake unto you out of the midst of the fire: ye heard the voice of the words, but saw no similitude; only ye heard a voice. And He declared unto you His covenant, which He commanded you to perform, even Ten Commandments; and He wrote them upon two tables of stone." Deuteronomy 4:11-13.

The covenant law which God proclaimed from Sinai reads as follows:

"God spake all these words, saying, . . .

1. Thou shalt have no other gods before Me.

2. Thou shalt not make unto thee any graven image, or any likeness of anything that is in heaven above, or that

is in the earth beneath, or that is in the water under the earth: thou shalt not bow down thyself to them, nor serve them: for I the Lord thy God am a jealous God, visiting the iniquity of the fathers upon the children unto the third and fourth generation of them that hate Me; and showing mercy unto thousands of them that love Me, and keep My commandments.

3. Thou shalt not take the name of the Lord thy God in vain; for the Lord will not hold him guiltless that taketh His name in vain.

4. Remember the Sabbath day, to keep it holy. Six days shalt thou labor, and do all thy work: but the seventh day is the Sabbath of the Lord thy God: in it thou shalt not do any work, thou, nor thy son, nor thy daughter, thy manservant, nor thy maidservant, nor thy cattle, nor thy stranger that is within thy gates: for in six days the Lord made heaven and earth, the sea, and all that in them is, and rested the seventh day: wherefore the Lord blessed the Sabbath day, and hallowed it.

5. Honor thy father and thy mother: that thy days may be long upon the land which the Lord thy God giveth thee.

6. Thou shalt not kill.

7. Thou shalt not commit adultery.

8. Thou shalt not steal.

9. Thou shalt not bear false witness against thy neighbor.

10. Thou shalt not covet thy neighbor's house, thou shalt not covet thy neighbor's wife, nor his manservant, nor his maidservant, nor his ox, nor his ass, nor anything that is thy neighbor's."

"These words the Lord spake unto all your assembly in the mount out of the midst of the fire, of the cloud, and of the thick darkness, with a great voice: and He added no more. And He wrote them in two tables of stone, and delivered them unto me." Deuteronomy 5:22.

"And I turned myself and came down from the mount, and put the tables in the ark which I had made; and there they be, as the Lord commanded me." Deuteronomy 10:5.

This law was endorsed by Christ in His Sermon on the Mount, and compliance with it was made a condition of salvation. Matthew 19:16-22; Mark 10:17-22; Luke 10: 25-28; 18:18-23.

From early Christian experience I had been taught that in religion there was no place for independent judgment, that I was not to use my mind, but trust in God and have faith. The advice was well meant and is largely true. We are to have faith, and we are saved by faith and not by works. But the suggestion that we are not to use our minds is entirely untrue. We are to serve God with our mind as well as with the other faculties. Hear these words of Christ: "And thou shalt love the Lord thy God with all thy heart, and with all thy soul, and with all thy mind, and with all thy strength: this is the first commandment. And the second is like, namely this, Thou shalt love thy neighbor as thyself. There is none other commandment greater than these." Mark 12:30, 31. See also Matthew 22: 37; Luke 10:27. As a fresh breath from heaven come the words, "Come now, and let us reason together, saith the Lord." Isaiah 1:18. Is it possible that God invites me to reason with Him? Paul supported the idea when he said, "Consider what I say; and the Lord give thee understanding in all things." 2 Timothy 2:7. "Consider" is defined: "To look at closely, to examine, to think about, to ponder in order to understand and decide, to observe, comprehend." Did Paul mean that I have a right to consider what he said? To think it over? And what did he mean when he said, "I speak as to wise men; *judge* ye what I say." 1 Corinthians 10:15. Perhaps we had expected to hear Paul say, "Swallow what I say." Instead of this he appealed to men's good sense, and told them to consider what he said. He was so sure of his grounds that he was willing to leave the decision with his hearers.

God is pleased when we use the mind He has given us and seriously consider a matter before taking action. Such is not an act of disbelief, but of intelligent faith. There must indeed be no doubtful hesitation in obeying God; but ordinarily He gives us time for reflection, that we may see light in His light and follow on to know the Lord.

Little children should be taught to obey without questioning. But as the child grows older, the wise parents will use a different method. They will spend time in explaining the reasons for certain requirements. And as the child gets the parent's viewpoint, there will be intelligent co-operation, unless the child is willfully stubborn.

It is thus God deals with us. He wants to reason with us; He wants us to consider, to judge. God treats us as grownups, which always appeals to a child. As we think matters through, we see wisdom in what might otherwise seem an arbitrary and unreasonable demand.

God could sit on His throne and issue His sovereign decrees without giving any reason for them. But He chooses the better way. He reveals His secrets to His servants, the prophets. Amos 3:7. He talked things over with Abraham before destroying Sodom and Gomorrah. Genesis 18:20-33. He would never dare give us the right to think, did He not know that when we have time to consider the matter, we will agree with Him. How can any fail to appreciate such a God! He makes us feel that we count. We are not mere automatons. Let no one misunderstand. God demands obedience. But He talks things over with us and leaves to us the final decision.

While, generally speaking, every request which God makes of us is a reasonable request, there are times when He tests us to see what we will do under certain circumstances. He tests us to see if we have learned to trust Him absolutely and if we will obey orders even without understanding them. Of such was the order to Simon Peter, "Launch out into the deep, and let down your nets for a draft." Luke 5:4. Christ was no fisherman, and Peter was. Also, Peter had been fishing all night and caught nothing, and in daylight it was no use to try again. Peter made a weak protest (verse 5), then let down the net, and the result was a greater catch than Peter had ever had before. This was Peter's first lesson in obedience. Years later when Christ told him to cast the net on the right side, there was no arguing. John 21:6. Peter could readily have argued that there were no more fish on the right side than on the left. But he had learned his lesson.

When Abraham was told to take his son Isaac and offer him on the mountain God should show him, he did not hesitate. Genesis 22:2, 3. He could not understand, but in previous years he had learned to trust God. Abraham stood the test for obedience.

These are interesting events, and there are others in the Bible. God likes to talk things over with His men, to prepare them for the time when there must be prompt and instant obedience.

God's Will in Me

It is well to pray that God's will be done in earth as it is in heaven, for that calls our minds to fields far and near where God's will is not being done or even known, and where we might be of some help. If we Christians pray this prayer, we cannot be inactive; for we have it in our power to help answer the prayer. When Christ said,

"This gospel of the kingdom shall be preached in all the world for a witness unto all nations; and then shall the end come" (Matthew 24:14), He was depending on us to do our part. He knew that such preaching was necessary if God's will was to be done. By our work with our neighbors, by our interest in fields afar, we may in a very definite way speed the day when God's will shall be done in the earth.

There is, however, a very personal application of this prayer that is of more importance than anything we can do for others. That is accepting God's will for ourselves. If we do this and our life becomes a God-directed life, He will be enabled to use us in ways we do not now understand or think possible. In the abstract it is easy to pray, "Thy will be done." Are we willing to make it personal?

It must have been a momentous disappointment for Moses when he was put aside and not permitted to enter the Promised Land and Joshua was given his place. He pleaded for permission to go in and see the land, but his prayer was denied. Deuteronomy 3:23-27. As for Joshua, said God to Moses, "encourage him, and strengthen him: for he shall go over before this people, and he shall cause them to inherit the land." Verse 28.

Moses bowed to the will of God, and on His behalf "he gave Joshua the son of Nun a charge, and said, Be strong and·of a good courage: for thou shalt bring the children of Israel into the land which I sware unto them: and I will be with thee." Deuteronomy 31:23. Moses did not enter the earthly Canaan; he died and God raised him from the grave in immortal glory.

Elijah must have been much discouraged when after the great day on Mount Carmel, where he did mighty exploits for God and won a signal victory, God rebuked him for his cowardly flight from Jezebel, and told him to put his mantle on Elisha. But he did not murmur. When he found Elisha, he "cast his mantle upon him." 1 Kings 19:19.

But God had not forsaken Elijah. He and Elisha worked together, until Elisha was fully able to take over the work. Then one day, as they walked along talking together, "behold, there appeared a chariot of fire, and horses of fire, and parted them both asunder; and Elijah went up by a whirlwind into heaven." 2 Kings 2:11. Elijah's work on earth was done; so God took him to heaven.

It must have been hard for Paul, the active and energetic one, to sit still in prison day after day and year after year. In the midst of a busy and useful life he was placed on the side lines, his work apparently done, though he was still in the strength of manhood and planning a world-wide work. Or was his work done? No, God was merely changing his work. He had been so busy traveling and preaching that he had not had time to do the writing God wanted done. There was yet a great deal of the New Testament to be written, and Paul was the man to do it. But he was too busy. He needed quietness and freedom from the care of the churches. So God arranged for him a time of quietness, and Paul immediately went to work. By writing fourteen of the twenty-seven books of the New Testament, he doubtless did more good than he did during his active ministry. Paul was willing to be set aside, and in his retirement he did a mighty work for God. He had learned in whatever state he was, therewith to be content.

What shall we say of John the Baptist? He had done a valiant work for God in preparing the way for Christ, and now that this work was done, he was consigned to prison and apparently forgotten. Did envy and jealousy fill his heart with discontent as a greater One had taken his place? No, a thousand times No. Said he, "He must increase, but I must decrease." John 3:30. Had Christ forgotten him? "Among them that are born of women there hath not risen a greater than John the Baptist." Matthew 11:11.

It is not easy to say, "Thy will be done," when one is set aside. But the men we have mentioned had learned the lesson. So Moses and Joshua appeared together, and Moses strengthened and encouraged Joshua. Elijah and Elisha walked and talked together, and the younger man was instructed by the older. Paul willingly changed his work and accomplished more than ever. And John cheerfully stepped aside when a greater than he appeared. All these accepted God's way, though it must have cost some of them great sorrow. All of them learned one of life's greatest lessons, to bow to disappointment, to say, "Thy will be done," and cheerfully do what God had for them to do. It is not easy to be set aside. But this is part of the program of life. He that can bow to the will of God, who can say from the heart, "Thy will be done," may be set at another task where he can still serve.

There may be those among the readers who have been set aside and resent it. Let us repeat: This is part of life, a lesson that all must learn. There may be wives who have been put aside and are passing through the experience of loneliness and of not being wanted. There may be grandparents who once had a happy home where all were welcome. Now they are given a rocking chair in a corner and are given to understand that they are not to make themselves too prominent when "company" comes. There are those who have held high office in state or church or institutions. Their counsel, which once was sought eagerly, is not in demand any more; they are outdated. The shock is almost unbearable for some persons.

It is easy enough to say that God's will be done, when all goes well. But it is not easy to say this when a loved one is on the deathbed and hope is gone. It is not easy to say it when we are personally involved, when we are incapacitated and feel we are in the way and our usefulness is at an end. It was not easy for Christ to say it in Gethsemane. But He did say it, and a world was saved.

Frustrations and disappointments are a part of life and an important part. For in the darkness God may be hid. If we relate ourselves rightly to reverses and "dis-appointments," they may become "His-appointments." If we accept the disappointments as ordered or permitted by God we may see God's will being done in our reaction. Therefore let all pray, "Thy will be done in me."

"Give Us This Day Our Daily Bread"

This petition does not ask for luxuries, but for bread, the barest necessities of life. The historian Gibbon, in recording one of the many famines in olden times, makes the observation that some of the delicate ladies in Rome learned for the first time how little it took to sustain life. They had feasted on nightingale's tongues and other delicacies, and now they were happy to get a crust of bread. This is a good lesson to learn. Paul says, "Having food and raiment let us be therewith content." 1 Timothy 6:8. God's promise does not include palatial homes, rich appointments, and all the latest conveniences. While we would not exclude these under appropriate circumstances, they are not included in Christ's prayer. In it we ask for bread.

God does not frown on riches. If we have honestly acquired some of the good things of life, and if we use them rightly, we may thank God for them. Job was the richest man in all the East, and God blessed him. Abraham was a rich man, and so were David and Solomon. God is not against riches, but against their misuse. Men who have riches and look down on others who have not, men who forget that it is God who gives power to obtain wealth and that they are not owners but stewards of their possessions, men who forget that a part of what they have God requires of them, men who forget their brother's need and close their eyes to the cry of the world—such will find it hard to enter heaven. It is easier for a camel to go through the eye of a needle than for them to gain eternal life. Matthew 19:24.

In daily bread we are justified in including not only bread to sustain life, but such things as shelter, clothing, health, and also food for the mind and, of course, spiritual needs. Many people in the world need bread, many are undernourished, and children suffer for want of that which we waste. A terrible responsibility rests upon those who have, who store up, who waste while others starve. This holds for nations and individuals. But great as the need is for temporal food, we must also admit that there is a great need for intellectual and spiritual nourishment. In some respects this need is even greater.

The prayer for bread furnishes an excellent illustration of how God answers prayer. We ask for bread, and then we work in the sweat of our face to provide it ourselves. Even though Christians believe in prayer, no one would think of asking God to furnish food without any effort on the part of the one who prays. Even when God sent manna from heaven, the Israelites had to go out and gather it. God did indeed send ravens with food for Elijah, and God can do the same today; but this is not God's ordinary way of working.

It is just as consistent to ask God for bread and expect

Him to bring it to our door, as to ask God for any other blessing and then sit back and wait for it, without raising a hand to help ourselves. The fact that we in most instances are to answer our own prayers needs to be impressed upon all. We may ask God to convert the heathen; but if so, we are not to look the other way when the collection plate is passed. God helps those who help themselves—and others.

To those who are religious but unconcerned about their brother's temporal needs, God sends a warning. "Cry aloud, spare not, lift up thy voice like a trumpet, and show My people their transgression, and the house of Jacob their sins. Yet they seek Me daily, and delight to know My ways, as a nation that did righteousness, and forsook not the ordinance of their God: they ask of Me the ordinances of justice; they take delight in approaching to God. Wherefore have we fasted, say they, and Thou seest not? wherefore have we afflicted our soul, and Thou takest no knowledge?" Isaiah 58:1-3.

The people who make the complaint that God takes no notice of them are religious people. They fast and afflict their souls, but God does not hear. They seek God daily and "delight in approaching to God." And still God does not hear their prayers. They think He ought to. They pray daily.

What is wrong with them? In His answer, God tells them wherein they fail. They pray and afflict their souls, they fast and keep the ordinances of God, but God ignores them. *They do not keep the right kind of fast.* Then God tells them what to do. They fast to be seen of men. They go with bowed heads and spread sackcloth and ashes under them. "Wilt thou call this a fast, and an acceptable day to the Lord?" asks God. Verse 5. Is not this the true fast, said God, "to deal thy bread to the hungry, and that thou bring the poor that are cast out to thy house [not to the poorhouse or some public institution]? when thou seest the naked, that thou cover him; and that thou hide not thyself from thine own flesh?" Verse 7. God's further demands are "to loose the bands of wickedness, to undo the heavy burdens, and to let the oppressed go free, and that ye break every yoke." Verse 6.

This calls for personal work for the needy and oppressed, not merely for a donation, even though it be liberal. It calls for social justice and the breaking of every yoke. Most of all, God wants His people to get in personal contact with the needs of the world. It is not enough to abstain from food when the larders are full. It is rather to empty the larders and give to the needy so that nothing is left for the giver himself. *That* is a fast in which God delights. There is no virtue in going without food when there is an abundance in the house. But to give *"thy* bread to the hungry"—that is real fasting.

If we do this, God promises many blessings. God will hear our prayers. "Then shalt thou call, and the Lord shall answer. . . . If thou draw out thy soul to the hungry, and satisfy the afflicted soul; then shall thy light rise in obscurity, and thy darkness be as the noonday: and the Lord shall guide thee continually, and satisfy thy soul in drought, and make fat thy bones: and thou shalt be like a watered garden, and like a spring of water, whose waters fail not." Isaiah 58:9-11.

In these verses God reveals some reasons why prayers are not answered. We have not considered the needs of others as we should. We have prided ourselves on what we have done, and cannot understand why God does not hear our prayers. Why does God not give more signal answers to our prayers? Why does He not hear our prayers for healing? Why does He not hear our prayers for conversions? Why are so many of our young people slipping away? Why are there so many divorces? Why is there such small attendance at the prayer meetings? Why, why, why, why? We have given, we have worked, we have prayed. Why does God not hear? It would be well to study carefully and prayerfully the fifty-eighth chapter of Isaiah. In that chapter there is light for God's people at this time. There is more religion in a loaf of bread and a bottle of milk than in the most profound lecture on predestination or in a discussion of the identity of the king of the north.

Christ mixed religion and practical Christianity. He preached to the people, and He fed the multitude. He did not prepare a banquet for them; He just gave them what was on hand, loaves and fishes. But they had enough and to spare. Matthew 15:32-39; 14:15-21. It may be supposed that many of those He fed were unworthy. They were more interested in the loaves and the fishes than in the preaching. John 6:26. But this did not deter Christ from feeding them; He ministered to the body as well as the soul.

Some will wonder why we should ask God for bread, when others do not ask and yet have as much as those who ask. In fact, some of those who do not ask have more than those who pray. Why, then, ask?

In asking for bread, we recognize our dependence upon God, not only for bread, but for our very existence. It is customary in accepting an invitation of hospitality to express our thanks to the host. Can we do less to God, the Giver of all good things? All may not thank God; but whether they do or not, God will send sunshine and rain, and through His divine alchemy transform the life of the seed into the life of a soul, capable of thinking, of willing, of doing, a candidate for immortality. Shall such bountiful liberality go unrecognized? If it is crude and boorish to neglect to thank a host, can it be any less to fail to thank God? However we treat Him, He will still provide for us. But he would appreciate being recognized as the Giver. As it is necessary to have food for the body, so also is it necessary to have food for the mind. Without physical food the body would shrivel up and death ensue. So with the mind. It needs proper food to prosper.

The human mind is a wonderful instrument. We need but to consider the inventions of the last few decades to have this demonstrated. Time and again men have wondered if the human race would not soon arrive at the ultimate, where there would be no new fields to explore, no more knowledge to be gained, no more things to be invented. That outlook has entirely changed. Men have now come to the point where they see unlimited work before them, vast fields that are calling for exploration. Their work is only well begun. With the conquering of Mount Everest, men began to look still higher and are now seriously considering communications with other worlds, and even visits to them. As in the days after the Flood, when men decided to build a tower that would reach to heaven, so men are having great celestial projects in mind. Why not create a few satellites and set them encircling the earth, constituting bases from which expeditions might be launched to reach some other planets? Will God permit men to go just so far, as He did in the days of the Tower of Babel, and then bring about confusion at the time when men are ready to climb to heaven? Genesis 11:1-9.

As science marches on and reveals the capacity of the human mind, the evil one is at work, turning much of the knowledge gained into destructive channels. Some sciences have been perverted so as to destroy faith in a

Creator, have substituted evolution for creation, and have made both the Creator and the Saviour seem unnecessary. Some men are making weapons to destroy mankind; others are propounding theories that destroy belief in God. It would seem that mankind is nearing the end of the road and that soon God will step in and take charge. It is high time for God to work.

Through the three great agencies of the press, radio, and television, information and knowledge are now being disseminated at an unprecedented pace. Their possibilities for good are almost unlimited, and the future may see even greater progress.

There are serious doubts, however, that present developments warrant an optimistic appraisal of their eventual value to society. A drastic change must take place. Can the coming generations, the children of today and the leaders of tomorrow, remain unaffected by the persistent portrayal of crime, lust, and murder? Can their intellectual diet of pulp magazines, cheap pornographic literature, corrupting novels, Sunday "funnies," and sex exposures develop the kind of fathers and mothers or leaders which the world needs? Is the screen justifying its existence as a builder of manhood and a trainer of citizens? The "legitimate" stage had this redeeming feature: The admission price was too high for children. But the screen has no such impediment. So we may see queues of children of tender age, waiting to be admitted to shows that should never see the light of day. Garbage is not good food for growing children, nor for adults.

It seems quite inconsistent for a government to enforce strict supervision over the food supply of a nation, by means of pure-food-and-drug departments and then permit men to fill the minds of the children with filth, swill from unclean reservoirs.

Has God given the church means to counteract this evil, at least as far as its own children are concerned, or are we helpless against these corrupting practices? Unless the church becomes fully awake to the danger of these modern inventions and takes adequate measures to save its children, the loss will be great. A world conflagration demands heroic countermeasures. To a prophet of old, sensing a crisis, came the message, "Let the priests, the ministers of the Lord, weep between the porch and the altar, and let them say, Spare Thy people, O Lord, and give not Thine heritage to reproach, that the heathen should rule over them: wherefore should they say among the people, Where is their God?" Joel 2:17.

The enemy has entered our homes; he is enthroned in the living rooms; he gathers the whole family together and shows them alluring pictures. He adapts his pictures to the mental capacities of the little ones, nor does he forget the older members. Mealtime is changed; bedtime is changed; the worship hour is adjusted; children refuse to eat or go to bed until they have seen their favorite production. All are entranced. A telephone call is an unwanted interruption; a visitor is a disturbance; all are immovable until the hour is past. And by that time all are unfitted for worship. Never before has such corruption been permitted in the homes, and never before has the danger to the young been so great. The time has come to weep between the porch and the altar, *and do something*. Who will show the way?

"Man shall not live by bread alone, but by every word that proceedeth out of the mouth of God." Matthew 4:4. Man needs daily bread to sustain life; he needs food for his mind; but most of all he needs spiritual food for his soul. He needs "the true bread from heaven." John 6:32. The Jews to whom Christ was speaking did not comprehend what He was saying; so He explained further: "The Bread of God is He which cometh down from heaven, and giveth life unto the world." "I am the Bread of Life: he that cometh to Me shall never hunger; and he that believeth on Me shall never thirst." John 6:33, 35. It is that bread of which Job says, "I have esteemed the words of His mouth more than my necessary food." Job 23:12.

The Jews still did not understand, so Christ explained further, "I am the living Bread which came down from heaven: if any man eat of this bread, he shall live forever: and the bread that I will give is My flesh, which I will give for the life of the world." John 6:51. "Many therefore of His disciples, when they had heard this, said, This is an hard saying; who can hear it?" "From that time many of His disciples went back, and walked no more with Him." Verses 60, 66.

It seems strange that many of His disciples had so little spiritual conception of Christ's word that they should become offended and walk no more with Him. Yet many today seem equally dull of perception. They are so engrossed in the things of this world that spiritual things are a closed book to them. Whether they know it or not, they need food for the soul even more than they need food for the body.

The Bible is our chief source of spiritual food. There are the green pastures and the still waters. There our soul may be restored. There the table is spread in the presence of enemies. There we may safely rest, and we will have no want.

We may find spiritual food at the Communion table, in the hour of divine worship, in quiet meditation and prayer. We may find it in the family circle as in morning and evening worship the incense of Christ's righteousness ascends with the prayer to the throne of God; we find it in the devotional books indited by God; we find it in reverent contemplation of God's handiwork in nature, in the heavens above and in the earth beneath. We find it in the communion of the saints, in ministry for the needy, at the bedside of a loved one. We find it as we face life's dark moments, as we give spiritual consolation to one entering the valley of the shadow of death.

For the devout soul there are spiritual values everywhere. And we may have them if we ask for them in the name of Him who taught us to pray, "Give us this day our daily bread."

The Bible is the most wonderful textbook in the world, adapted to all classes of people everywhere. The untutored aborigines and the learned scholar can there find spiritual food and consolation. In it can be found the A B C of godliness and also the deepest and most profound problems of existence. It is a textbook that can never be exhausted. In school we may graduate from one class to another and find a little harder textbook as we advance. In the Bible we also advance, but the textbook is the same, miraculously adapted to every man, whatever his standing or attainment. While the practice of some to read the Bible through as often as possible is commendable and much good may be gained, this should not be the ordinary or only procedure. It is like going through the country in an automobile at sixty miles an hour and viewing the landscape. This is good, and a general bird's-eye view may be had and much of beauty seen. But it is well to stop once in a while and get out and look at the flowers, a waterfall, a Grand Canyon, a cliff dwelling, a dam, a secluded valley, or the "Great White Throne." It is well to rest awhile in the cool shade of the majestic trees from of old, or delight in the bloom of the desert.

We are not depreciating the practice of reading the

Bible through even many times. But neither must we miss the joy of finding a rose in the desert, or the beauty of heaven in a little lake, or the sweet companionship of saints as we journey along.

In Paul's letter to the Hebrews he took the believers to task for not studying as they ought. "When for the time ye ought to be teachers, ye have need that one teach you again which be the first principles of the oracles of God; and are become such as have need of milk, and not of strong meat." Hebrews 5:12.

This was a serious rebuke to the church. "Ye ought to be teachers." This may be true of many today. They have not improved their talent, have not advanced in the truth as they ought. They have need of milk, when they should be ready for more solid food.

"Everyone that useth milk is unskillful in the word of righteousness." Verse 13. There is indeed a "sincere milk of the word;" but it is for babes, "that ye may grow thereby." 1 Peter 2:2. A little babe is wonderful, but a sixty-year-old babe is not. Such an one needs to be weaned and learn to feed himself and masticate his food, not depending on others to do it for him. If he is ever to grow up he must learn to tackle hard problems in his study. Note these instructions:

"The study of the Bible demands our most diligent effort and persevering thought. As the miner digs for the golden treasure in the earth, so earnestly, persistently, must we seek for the treasure of God's word.

"In daily study the verse-by-verse method is often most helpful. Let the student take one verse, and concentrate the mind on ascertaining the thought that God has put into that verse for him, and then dwell upon the thought until it becomes his own. One passage thus studied until its significance is clear is of more value than the perusal of many chapters with no definite purpose in view and no positive instruction gained."—*Education,* page 189.

"Everyone should seek to understand the great truths of the plan of salvation, that he may be ready to give an answer to everyone who asks the reason of his hope. You should know what caused the fall of Adam, so that you may not commit the same error, and lose heaven as he lost Paradise. You should study the lives of patriarchs and prophets, and the history of God's dealing with men in the past; for these things were 'written for our admonition, upon whom the ends of the world are come.' We should study the divine precepts, and seek to comprehend their depth. We should meditate upon them until we discern their importance and immutability. We should study the life of our Redeemer, for He is the only perfect example for men. We should contemplate the infinite sacrifice of Calvary, and behold the exceeding sinfulness of sin and the righteousness of the law. You will come from a concentrated study of the theme of redemption strengthened and ennobled. Your comprehension of the character of God will be deepened; and with the whole plan of salvation clearly defined in your mind, you will be better able to fulfill your divine commission."—*Review and Herald,* April 24, 1888, p. 258.

God has provided an abundance of spiritual food for all. But we must gather the manna; we must assimilate the truths revealed. As we do so we help fulfill the prayer, "Give us this day our daily bread."

"Forgive Us Our Debts"

When Christ took our sins upon Himself, died, and thus paid our debt, we became indebted to Him. The price He paid for our redemption was so great that we can never repay it. And He does not expect us to. But

He does expect us to recognize it and express our willingness to do all we can to show our appreciation. Moreover, on some of the gifts He has given us He requires that we pay interest.

In his letter to the Corinthians, Paul enunciated a principle according to which God works, and which is most comforting. Said he, "If there be first a willing mind, it is accepted according to that a man hath, and not according to that he hath not." 2 Corinthians 8:12.

Paul had been collecting money for the poor in Jerusalem. A year had passed, and some of the pledges were not yet paid. He encouraged them to finish the task, saying, "Now therefore perform the doing of it;" that is, pay up, "that as there was a readiness to will, so there may be a performance also *out of that which ye have.*" Verse 11. They had been slow in paying, and even now some were unable to pay all they had promised; but, said he, pay "out of that which ye have;" that is: If you cannot pay the whole sum now, pay what you can, and it will be "accepted according to that a man hath, and not according to that he hath not." This was most liberal and gracious.

In harmony with this statement is the following quotation, given also elsewhere: "When it is in the heart to obey God, when efforts are put forth to this end, Jesus accepts this disposition and effort as man's best service, and He makes up for the deficiency with His own divine merit."—Ellen G. White, *Signs of the Times,* June 16, 1890.

While we can never pay the debt we owe, we can recognize it and make known to the world that the debt is paid for us and for them, "that God was in Christ, reconciling the world unto Himself, not imputing their trespasses unto them; and hath committed unto us the word of reconciliation. Now then we are ambassadors for

Christ, as though God did beseech you by us: we pray you in Christ's stead, be ye reconciled to God. For He hath made Him to be sin for us, who knew no sin; that we might be made the righteousness of God in Him." 2 Corinthians 5:19-21.

"As We Forgive Our Debtors"

The great debt we owe to God was incurred in the forgiveness of sin which necessitated the death of Christ on the cross. "All have sinned." Romans 3:23. This means that *we* have sinned, that *I* have sinned. In His fathomless love God forgave us all, and we are free from condemnation and have passed from death unto life. Should not this fill our hearts with thanksgiving and joy?

But there is one important condition on which this forgiveness depends: We are forgiven our sins only as we forgive others fully and freely. God has forgiven us; now we are to forgive others. "If ye forgive men their trespasses, your heavenly Father will also forgive you: but if ye forgive not men their trespasses, neither will your Father forgive your trespasses." Matthew 6:14, 15.

This forgiveness is to be extended to those who have offended us, whether they ask for forgiveness or not. If they do not come to us to ask forgiveness, we are to go to them. "If thou bring thy gift to the altar, and there rememberest that thy brother hath aught against thee [not that *you* have aught against him]; leave there thy gift before the altar, and go thy way; first be reconciled to thy brother, and then come and offer thy gift." Matthew 5:23, 24. "If you have committed one wrong and they twenty, confess that one as though you were the chief offender."—Ellen G. White, *Review and Herald,* Dec. 16, 1884.

Once Peter asked Christ how often he should forgive

his brother. To this Jesus answered, "Until seventy times seven." Matthew 18:21, 22. Jesus then spoke a parable about forgiveness, emphasizing that forgiveness of our own sins depends on our forgiving those who have sinned against us.

"Therefore is the kingdom of heaven likened unto a certain king, which would take account of his servants. And when he had begun to reckon, one was brought unto him, which owed him ten thousand talents. But forasmuch as he had not to pay, his lord commanded him to be sold, and his wife, and children, and all that he had, and payment to be made. The servant therefore fell down, and worshiped him, saying, Lord, have patience with me, and I will pay thee all. Then the lord of that servant was moved with compassion, and loosed him, and forgave him the debt. But the same servant went out, and found one of his fellow servants, which owed him an hundred pence: and he laid hands on him, and took him by the throat, saying, Pay me that thou owest. And his fellow servant fell down at his feet, and besought him, saying, Have patience with me, and I will pay thee all. And he would not: but went and cast him into prison, till he should pay the debt. So when his fellow servants saw what was done, they were very sorry, and came and told unto their lord all that was done. Then his lord, after that he had called him, said unto him, O thou wicked servant, I forgive thee all that debt, because thou desirest me: shouldest not thou also have had compassion on thy fellow servant, even as I had pity on thee? And his lord was wroth, and delivered him to the tormentors, till he should pay all that was due unto him. So likewise shall My heavenly Father do also unto you, if ye from your hearts forgive not everyone his brother their trespasses." Matthew 18:23-35.

No one can misunderstand the lesson of this parable.

The servant who had been forgiven much showed an unforgiving and cruel attitude toward the one who owed him a small sum; and though he had already been forgiven and his great debt marked paid, the judgment was reversed and he was condemned to pay all that he owed. This parable teaches clearly that we are forgiven only as we forgive, and that it is useless to ask to have our sins forgiven unless we "from the heart" forgive those who have sinned against us.

God has entrusted to all men one or more talents for which we are held responsible. They constitute a debt on which He expects us to pay interest. This is clearly taught in this parable:

"For the kingdom of heaven is as a man traveling into a far country, who called his own servants, and delivered unto them his goods. And unto one he gave five talents, to another two, and to another one; to every man according to his several ability; and straightway took his journey. Then he that had received the five talents went and traded with the same, and made them other five talents. And likewise he that had received two, he also gained other two. But he that had received one went and digged in the earth, and hid his lord's money. After a long time the lord of those servants cometh, and reckoneth with them. And so he that had received five talents came and brought other five talents, saying, Lord, thou deliveredst unto me five talents: behold, I have gained beside them five talents more. His lord said unto him, Well done, thou good and faithful servant: thou hast been faithful over a few things, I will make thee ruler over many things: enter thou into the joy of thy lord. He also that had received two talents came and said, Lord, thou deliveredst unto me two talents: behold, I have gained two other talents beside them. His lord said unto him, Well done, good and faithful servant; thou hast been faithful over a few things, I will make thee ruler over many things: enter thou into the joy of thy lord. Then he which had received the one talent came and said, Lord, I knew thee that thou art an hard man, reaping where thou hast not sown, and gathering where thou hast not strawed: and I was afraid, and went and hid thy talent in the earth: lo, there thou hast that is thine. His lord answered and said unto him, Thou wicked and slothful servant, thou knewest that I reap where I sowed not, and gathered where I have not strawed: thou oughtest therefore to have put my money to the exchangers, and then at my coming I should have received mine own with usury. Take therefore the talent from him, and give it unto him which hath ten talents. For unto everyone that hath shall be given, and he shall have abundance: but from him that hath not shall be taken away even that which he hath. And cast ye the unprofitable servant into outer darkness: there shall be weeping and gnashing of teeth." Matthew 25:14-30.

In the parable he that received five talents gained other five, and he was told, "Well done." Each had been given the number of talents he could use, "according to his several ability." The Lord did not expect a return of five talents from the one who had been given two. On the other hand, He would not have been satisfied with a return of two talents from the one who had been given five.

The man who had received one talent did not attempt to improve it, but buried it in the earth. We are not told the reason for his failure to trade with it. He might have thought that it was small and did not matter. He might have been discontented with receiving only one talent when others received more. From the fact that he called the master a hard man, we may presume that he felt unjustly treated. Had he improved his one talent, he doubtless would have received another one, with the commendation of the master, "Well done."

The excuse he gave was, "I knew thee that thou art an hard man. . . . And I was afraid, and went and hid thy talent in the earth: lo, there thou hast that is thine." This was a lame excuse. Had he really thought that the Lord was a hard master, should he not have been the more anxious to get his good will by paying him back with interest? He was not acting wisely.

What are these talents? They are the skills with which God has endowed men, the inclinations, the capacities, the aptitudes which make one man a poet, another an author, another a preacher, another a carpenter, another a counselor, another a watchmaker. As related to the church, one has the gift of song, another of playing instrumental music, another of storytelling for the children, another of teaching a class, another of doing Dorcas work, another of visiting, another of arranging flowers, another of giving "chalk talks." One who may not be able to sing a solo can join the choir and do his part. Everyone can do something. Everyone has at least one talent. And note: It was the one who had only one talent who did not use it and hence lost it. So let the one-talent man beware! Let him not bury his talent. If he has done so, let him dig it up and use it. It is not enough to be a church member. Everyone can do something, however lowly the task, and be blessed in doing it. As he does the best he can, as a reward God may give him another talent, which will increase his work and also his blessings.

In 1 Corinthians 12:8-11, Paul gives this list of talents:

"To one is given by the Spirit the word of wisdom; to another the word of knowledge by the same Spirit; to another faith by the same Spirit; to another the gifts of

healing by the same Spirit; to another the working of miracles; to another prophecy; to another discerning of spirits; to another divers kinds of tongues; to another the interpretation of tongues: but all these worketh that one and the selfsame Spirit, dividing to every man severally as He will."

Later in the same chapter he says this:

"God hath set some in the church, first apostles, secondarily prophets, thirdly teachers, after that miracles, then gifts of healings, helps, governments, diversities of tongues. Are all apostles? are all prophets? are all teachers? are all workers of miracles? Have all the gifts of healing? do all speak with tongues? do all interpret? But covet earnestly the best gifts: and yet show I unto you a more excellent way." Verses 28-31.

Among the great gifts here mentioned, note the little word "helps." There are some who are not gifted to lead out in various enterprises, but are excellent help. They may not think they are doing anything vital, just "helping along." But that may be very important at times. We are constantly hearing the call for leaders, and these are needed. But it is just as true that we need followers, men who are willing to fill in, playing "second fiddle," doing small menial tasks that need to be done. For a while Elisha, who later became a great prophet, did little else than pour "water on the hands of Elijah." 2 Kings 3:11. But not long after, Elijah's mantle fell on him, and he received a double portion of God's Spirit. 2 Kings 2:9.

"Every man shall receive *his own reward* according to his own labor." 1 Corinthians 3:8. This means that every man can determine his own reward, and that this will be according to his work. He can determine to do a great work in his line, and receive a great reward; or to do but little, and receive a small reward. Let no one, therefore,

bury his talent. Do not evade responsibility. If you are asked to take a position, consider the matter. Someone has confidence in you that you can do the work or soon grow into it. Pray over it, but be sure your prayers are not biased. And be sure not to bury your talent in the ground, however small the talent may seem.

Christians are in debt to the world in a sense different from that which we have discussed. Of this Paul said, "I am debtor both to the Greeks, and to the barbarians; both to the wise, and to the unwise. So, as much as in me is, I am ready to preach the gospel to you that are at Rome also." Romans 1:14, 15.

Every Christian ought to do his share of the world's work. He ought to be a good citizen, obey the law, honor the government, pay his taxes, and take part in endeavors he can honestly support. There are too many of these for him to be active in all, but he can choose one or more and do his honest share.

The Bible direction is: "To do your own business, and to work with your own hands, as we commanded you." 1 Thessalonians 4:11. In his next letter he added, "This we commanded you, that if any would not work, neither should he eat." That is, Christians should not "live on" others, as some evidently tried to do in Thessalonica. Paul was not in the habit of commanding his hearers. But in this instance he commanded that if any will not work, neither should he eat. Christians must justify the protection they get from the government. They must do their part in every good word and work.

But aside from this civil responsibility, they owe a debt to the world, of which Paul spoke when he said he was a debtor to all men. The Christian has something the world does not have, the gospel, and this he should share with them.

Paul felt keenly the burden of that debt. He knew what awaited him in Rome: opposition, imprisonment, death; but this did not deter him. He owed Rome a debt, and he must pay it, whatever it might mean to him personally. So Paul went to Rome.

We owe a debt as verily as did Paul. This accounts for foreign missions. Paul did not confine his work to his own circle. He had a world vision. He took Isaiah's statement literally, that it was too light a thing for him to minister to Israel only, "to restore the preserved of Israel," to minister to those who already were in the church. God said, "I will also give thee for a light to the Gentiles, that thou mayest be My salvation unto the end of the earth." Isaiah 49:6. Paul accepted this responsibility.

Applying this principle to the situation today, we find ourselves confronted with a world task. Under these conditions it is too light a thing that we should confine our work to our own neighborhood. It is well that we have revivals "to restore the preserved of Israel." But we must not devote an undue portion of our time to work of that nature. We must lift up our eyes and view the field. The gospel must be sent to all the world, and precious talent must not be confined to hover over the churches. We cannot all go to fields afar, but we can all sacrifice; we can all pray. To such as cannot go but gladly would if circumstances permitted, this precious promise is given, that "as his part is that goeth down to the battle, so shall his part be that tarrieth by the stuff: they shall part alike." 1 Samuel 30:24. Blessed be God.

There are many who would gladly go into public work if they were free to do so. But home duties hold them. There are faithful mothers and wives who must stay at home and are deprived of the joy of assisting their husbands in soul-saving work. Let them be of good courage.

The Lord understands. He promises that those who tarry by the stuff shall share with them that go down to the battle. Wonderful promise! If we get forgiveness for our sins only upon condition that we forgive them that trespass against us, the first thing we must do before we ask forgiveness is to examine our own hearts to ascertain if there are those we have not forgiven. As is noted above, we are not to wait until they come to us. We are to go to them. Matthew 5:23, 24. Christ considered this so important that He said we are to leave our gift at the altar and go first to see the brother, and then bring the gift.

God commends prayer, and He would have all men pray. But there are times when prayer must wait. Go *first,* He said, and be reconciled with thy brother. If all followed this advice, there would be love and harmony in the church, and Christ's promise would be fulfilled, that "If ye have love one to another," then "shall all men know that ye are My disciples." John 13:35.

Let the mind dwell for a moment on this promise. We all desire to convince the world of the truths we hold. We like to have them be convinced that there is a people who have God's approval, that have the truth for this time. Can we ever do this? Yes. "By this shall all men know that ye are My disciples, if ye have love one to another." This is the test.

This makes our duty and our privilege clear. I must go to every brother with whom I am at variance and become reconciled to him. I must do this to have my own sins forgiven, and I must do this to convince the world that I belong with the people of God.

It is a sad commentary on our Christianity that God finds it necessary to remind us daily that we are to put out of our hearts all malice and hatred if we expect to receive God's pardon. No Christian has any right to pray the

Lord's Prayer if he harbors resentment against any. If he nevertheless prays, he stands self-convicted by his own prayer, for he asks only that God will forgive him as he forgives. Let us therefore ask God to help us pray rightly, "Forgive us our debts, as we forgive our debtors."

"Lead Us Not Into Temptation"

"Let no man say when he is tempted, I am tempted of God: for God cannot be tempted with evil, neither tempteth He any man." James 1:13. If God does not tempt, who does?

Satan does. "Then was Jesus led up of the Spirit into the wilderness to be tempted of the devil." Matthew 4:1. "He was there in the wilderness forty days, tempted of Satan." Mark 1:13.

Man tempts himself. "Every man is tempted, when he is drawn away of his own lust, and enticed." James 1:14. Satan, however, is the originator of man's temptations. He presents some alluring temptation to man, and man falls into the trap.

It should be noted that the Bible also states that God tempts. "It came to pass after these things, that God did tempt Abraham." Genesis 22:1. Is this statement a contradiction of what James says above, that God does not tempt? that "God cannot be tempted with evil, neither tempteth He any man"?

We think not. James speaks of being tempted with *evil*. The reading therefore demands that as God cannot be tempted with evil, neither does He tempt any man with *evil*. Note also, that the statement that God tempted Abraham, in the margin has the reading, "God did *prove* Abraham." Paul, recording the event, said, "By faith Abraham, when he was tried, offered up Isaac." Hebrews 11:17.

The Hebrew word for "tempt" in Genesis 22:1 is defined, "test, put to the test, tempt, try, prove." An example of the word used is found in the record of Hezekiah's sickness, when he made the mistake of showing all his riches to the ambassadors from Babylon. The record reads that God "left him, to try him." 2 Chronicles 32:31. The word "try" is the same Hebrew word translated "tempt" in Genesis 22:1.

Tests and trial are necessary for God's people. Adam and Eve were tested in the Garden of Eden. They failed. Job also was tested. He stood the test. Said Job, "He knoweth the way that I take: when He hath tried me, I shall come forth as gold." Job 23:10. Abraham also stood the test; so did Christ.

God tests His people to make them stronger, to develop in them powers of resistance. Daniel observed, "Some of them of understanding shall fall, to try them, and to purge, and to make them white." Daniel 11:35. "Many shall be purified, and made white, and tried." Daniel 12:10. This kind of test and trial is entirely different from Satan's temptation which he brings on for the purpose of enticing men to sin. Job knew that he would come forth from the trial as gold. Daniel said that those who stand the test will be purified and made white. On the contrary, when Satan tempts, he hopes to cause men to sin. God tries men to make them strong, to resist Satan's temptations.

When God tests a man and brings him into temptation, or gives the evil one permission to do so, He closely watches Satan that he does not go beyond the line God has set. Satan may go just so far and no farther. Paul puts it well when he says that God "will not suffer you to be tempted above that ye are able; but will with the temptation also make a way to escape, *that ye may be able to bear it.*" 1 Corinthians 10:13. God knows how much we

can bear, and He will not permit Satan to go above the
limit. He will see us through, if we will but trust Him.
As Satan brings on one trial after another, God watches
carefully. And at the precise moment He will say, "Stop."
And Satan obeys.

As stated above, trials are necessary for God's people
if they are to acquire the necessary strength for complete
victory over sin. At this time in the world's history trials
are necessary to prepare us for the coming events that will
try men to the utmost. God's promise is, "Because thou
hast kept the word of My patience, I also will keep thee
from the hour of temptation, which shall come upon all
the world, to try them that dwell upon the earth." Revelation 3:10. "The devil shall cast some of you into prison,
that ye may be tried." Revelation 2:10. But the glorious
promise is made, "As thy days, so shall thy strength be."
Deuteronomy 33:25. "Blessed is the man that endureth
temptation: for when he is tried, he shall receive the crown
of life." James 1:12. It was with this in mind that James
could say, "My brethren, count it all joy when ye fall into
divers temptations; knowing this, that the trying of your
faith worketh patience. But let patience have her perfect
work, that ye may be perfect and entire, wanting nothing." Verses 2-4.

What, then, is the meaning of the prayer when we are
to ask God not to bring us into temptation? We accept
Paul's explanation when he says that while God will permit us to be tempted, He will not permit Satan to tempt
us above what we are able to bear. 1 Corinthians 10:13.
The prayer means that we are to ask God for strength
to bear what He has for us, that we may not sink beneath
the load. In the midst of the trial, when it seems that we
can bear no more, we are to remember that God keeps
watch over us, that He also watches Satan, and that He

will permit just so much and no more. We may be sure
that God is at our side and will not forsake us. In the dark
hours we may look to God in faith and assure ourselves
that "when He hath tried me, I shall come forth as gold."
Job 23:10.

When we are passing through trials we know that we
are in the hands of God, that He is observing us and is
carefully measuring each stroke. We know that His purpose is to try us, to purge us, and to make us white. Daniel
11:35. We are to pray for the necessary strength to bear
what God permits and to have faith that He will find the
way of escape, as He has promised.

When Christ came to the hour of His great trial, He
"offered up prayers and supplications with strong crying
and tears unto Him that was able to save Him from death,
and was heard in that He feared." Hebrews 5:7. Christ
did not ask to be saved from death, as some think, but
prayed to Him who was *able* to save Him. Had Christ
asked to be saved from death, then the statement that He
was heard could not be true, for He was not saved from
death. He died. What He wanted was assurance of the
certainty of a resurrection, of victory over death, of assurance that the separation from His Father would not be
eternal. In this prayer He was heard.

This view finds support in the fact that the Greek "save
from death" is literally "save out of death." Christ had
become man. He was now about to enter the domain of
Satan, who "had the power of death." Hebrews 2:14.
Would the devil be able to hold Him in this death He
was to die? Christ wanted to make sure. The psalmist
had expressed an assurance: "My flesh also shall rest in
hope. For Thou wilt not leave my soul in hell; neither
wilt Thou suffer Thine Holy One to see corruption."
Psalm 16:9, 10. When Christ received this assurance that

He would be raised again, His prayer "was heard in that He feared." Hebrews 5:7.

The prayer, "Lead us not into temptation," may therefore be interpreted to mean, "Lead us not into any temptation harder than we can bear." This prayer is according to God's promise, and will therefore be heard. When we are in the midst of some great trial we are to remember this promise and this prayer and are to say: "Lord, Thou hast promised not to make the trial harder than I can bear. I seem to be almost at the breaking point, but I have faith, Lord, that Thou knowest best. If Thou seest that I can bear a little more, I believe Thy word and trust in Thy strength. Lord, 'Thy will be done.'"

"Lead us not into temptation," is a prayer of trust and faith in God. It is not "Save me from this hour," but "Keep me in this hour."

"Deliver Us From Evil"

Instead of "Deliver us from evil," some translate, "Deliver us from the evil one." Since both readings are permissible, and since the difference in this case does not seem vital, we accept both readings. We wish deliverance from evil, and also from the evil one.

This is not a petition for forgiveness. That is covered in the prayer, "Forgive us our debts." Nor is it merely a prayer for deliverance from accidents and other evils that threaten us everywhere, but deliverance from evil that lurks in the heart—evil thoughts, evil words, evil deeds. It is a prayer for complete sanctification, deliverance from all evil, power to overcome and live a holy life. It is a prayer of one who wishes to heed the command, "Go, and sin no more."

We are convinced that Christians do not make the distinction between forgiveness *of* sin and deliverance *from* sin, that should be made. Forgiveness of sin operates *after* the sin has been committed; deliverance operates before, or rather it so operates that the sin will not be committed. It will keep a man from sinning rather than wait until the sin has been done and then forgive it. It is the power of which Jude speaks when he says that God is *"able to keep you from falling,* and to present you faultless before the presence of His glory with exceeding joy." Jude 24.

An illustration may here be to the point. Years ago I heard a dialogue between two children. They were discussing what should be done with the money collected in the Sabbath school. Should they use it for erecting a fence, or should they buy an ambulance? To me it seemed nonsense, for they had not enough money for either. After a while I began to understand what they were after. They were telling of their playground which was on a high hill with one side that was very steep. Some of the children had gone too near the edge, and one had fallen down and broken a leg. Now the question was: To prevent further injury should they get an ambulance, or should they erect a fence? They decided they needed both, but that they might dispense with the ambulance after they got the fence.

This childish story conveys a deep lesson for Christians. It is wonderful to be forgiven. It is still more wonderful to be kept from sinning. It is wonderful to have an ambulance to take the injured to the place where help can be found. It is still more wonderful to have a fence that will keep them from falling. Spiritually, forgiveness is wonderful; the greater power of God to keep from falling is still more wonderful.

Let no one suppose that we are thinking lightly of forgiveness. It is surpassingly glorious that God can and will forgive, even though we sin time and again. Said the psalmist, "Blessed is he whose transgression is forgiven, whose sin is covered. Blessed is the man unto whom the Lord imputeth not iniquity, and in whose spirit there is no guile." Psalm 32:1, 2. It is a blessed experience to have our sins forgiven and covered, and to be clothed "with the garments of salvation." Romans 4:7; Isaiah 61:10.

God illustrates this wonderful experience in the parable of the prodigal son whose father, on the homecoming of the son, commanded, "Bring forth the best robe, and put it on him; and put a ring on his hand, and shoes on his feet." Luke 15:22. In a moment's time the rags were all covered, and the evidence of his former condition hid. The father's robe covered all.

This is symbolic of what happens at conversion. The sinner comes to God, "wretched, and miserable, and poor, and blind, and naked." Revelation 3:17. But God covers him with the garment of salvation, clothes him with the robe of righteousness. His sins are forgiven and covered. He has done nothing to deserve this; it is all of grace. God counts him righteous though he is still not righteous. His sins are forgiven, but they are still there, though covered. He has started on the right road, and God imputes to him "righteousness without works." Romans 4:6. His sins are forgiven, but the work is not finished. The sins must be eradicated, not merely covered. This work of eradication of sin is the work of sanctification, and it eventuates in holiness. This is not the work of a moment, or of a year, but of a lifetime. It begins, or should begin, at conversion. The man has been a drunkard. Now he stops drinking. He has been immoral. Now he begins to live a moral life. He has not always told the truth. Now he becomes truthful. He has not been honest. Now he starts a new life. Each separate step is an advance toward sanctification. He does not commit adultery and then ask God for forgiveness. He does not steal and then beg pardon. These former things have passed away. He is a new creature in Christ Jesus. He has not yet attained; he is not already perfect. But with Paul he follows after. Philippians 3:12. He is "perfecting holiness in the fear of God." 2 Corinthians 7:1. He is on the right road, and though he may not have attained, God counts him righteous, and he will have the crown of life though he may yet be far from the perfect standard.

This experience is what some call "the victorious life," which does not mean perfection or even a life above sin. For sin may overtake such a one, but though he fall he will rise again. "A just man falleth seven times, and riseth up again." Proverbs 24:16. Here some well-meaning persons may make a mistake. They have been taught that a Christian does not sin, and *that* is good doctrine. But they have also been taught that if they do sin, they are no longer Christians. This is not true. Said the beloved disciple, "My little children, these things write I unto you, that ye sin not. And if any man sin, we have an advocate with the Father, Jesus Christ the righteous: and He is the propitiation for our sins: and not for ours only, but also for the sins of the whole world." 1 John 2:1, 2. John warned us not to sin. But he did not say that if we sin we are lost and are no more Christians. He said that we still have an advocate.

The road of sanctification is a long road, but one of continual progress. Little by little the sinner gains the victory over sin. As far as he has come, so far he is sanctified. He does not sin and carouse. He walks softly before God. He has come a long way, but he has not as yet perfected holiness. With Paul he confesses: "not as though I had already attained, either were already perfect. . . .

Brethren, I count not myself to have apprehended: but this one thing I do, forgetting those things which are behind, and reaching forth unto those things which are before, *I press toward the mark* for the prize of the high calling of God in Christ Jesus. Let us therefore, as many as be perfect, be thus minded." Philippians 3:12-15.

We have come to the time when God is ready to make a demonstration of what He can do in human flesh. He proposes to present to the world a people without spot or blemish or any such thing, a people that can stand in the sight of a holy God without an intercessor. Such a demonstration is long overdue. Long enough has Satan challenged God to produce such a people, and has sneeringly asked, "Where are they that keep the commandments of God and the faith of Jesus?" God will then produce them and say, "Here they are."

In the 144,000, God will show that by His grace men can meet the standard He has set. Satan will claim that the demonstration is possible only because God shields them, and that if he were given permission to test them, they would fall. He is given that permission, and this is what will bring on the time of Jacob's trouble. The saints will be tried to the utmost. It will seem at times that they can endure no longer; but they will not fail. With Job they will say, "Though He slay me, yet will I trust in Him." Job 13:15. God will stand justified in His saints. In them He demonstrates that men *can* keep the commandments of God under the most trying circumstances, that the weakest of the weak can do it, even with death staring them in the face. They demonstrate that if this can be done with Satan bringing all his power to bear on them to yield, there is no excuse for any ever to have failed. They justify God in His sayings.

To be delivered from evil means deliverance from sin,

full and complete deliverance; it means sanctification perfected. For this demonstration "the whole creation groaneth and travaileth in pain together until now." Romans 8:22. "The earnest expectation of the creature [margin, "creation"] waiteth for the manifestation of the sons of God," waits for the coming of that group that will reflect the image of Jesus fully. Verse 19. They will stand at last upon the sea of glass, "having His Father's name written in their foreheads." Revelation 14:1. "I saw as it were a sea of glass mingled with fire: and them that had gotten the victory over the beast, and over his image, and over his mark, and over the number of his name, stand on the sea of glass, having the harps of God. And they sing the song of Moses the servant of God, and the song of the Lamb, saying, Great and marvelous are Thy works, Lord God Almighty; just and true are Thy ways, Thou King of saints." Revelation 15:2, 3.

These have prayed the Lord's Prayer. They have asked to be delivered from evil and the evil one. And deliverance has come. They stand victorious on the sea of glass.

On this high note of holiness and sanctification ends the last petition in the Lord's Prayer. Deliverance from evil, victory over every besetment—perfected holiness is the goal of God for man. And now it is reached. God has made His demonstration; Satan has been given his last chance to destroy God's people. He retires defeated from this last conflict. God has conquered.

"Thine Is the Kingdom, and the Power, and the Glory"

Luke omitted this entire doxology, and the American Revised Version omits it also in Matthew. As it is not found in the older manuscripts, it may be a later addition. However, as there is an introduction to the prayer, it seems fitting that there should also be a close. Without such a close, the prayer ends abruptly. As it is a beautiful and dignified ascription to God, and as Christendom in general has adopted it, we do the same.

In the Scriptures God gives to Christ all the glory; and likewise Christ gives to the Father all honor. There appears to be a most beautiful courtesy in the Godhead. In these closing sentences of the Lord's Prayer, Christ gives all power and glory to the Father, while in the first chapter of Hebrews God gives all glory to the Son. As we have noted in our remarks of the prayer, Christ informs us that He does nothing of Himself. The Father tells Him what to do and say, and the Son does it. In the first chapter of Hebrews, God, the Father, calls His Son both Lord and God and commands the angels to worship Him. And so throughout the Bible.

In this closing section of the Lord's Prayer, Christ gives the Father all glory and power, and says that to Him belongs the kingdom. We join Him in giving God the glory.

25

With God in the Dark

WHO is among you that feareth the Lord, that obeyeth the voice of His servant, that walketh in darkness, and hath no light? let him trust in the name of the Lord, and stay upon his God." Isaiah 50:10.

These words are written for the faithful soul who is passing through the dark hours that come to everyone bound for the kingdom. The one addressed "feareth the Lord," "obeyeth the voice of His servant," yet "walketh in darkness, and hath no light." He is not, then, an unbeliever or apostate. He fears the Lord and obeys God's servant. He prays, but receives no answer; he is in the dark as to the next step he shall take; he does not know what to do.

Such experiences come to every believing soul, and he is perplexed. What shall he do? The answer is prompt. "Let him trust in the name of the Lord, and stay upon his God." That is, do not give up; trust God that *He* knows; learn to walk with God in the dark as well as in the light. Clasp His hand a little tighter. All will come out right.

This was Christ's experience in Gethsemane. There all was oppressive gloom, and not a ray of light came through.

He was in bewilderment as well as agony; the Father's face was hidden. Christ was facing the darkness of the tomb, and hope did not assure Him that He would come from the grave a conqueror or tell Him that the Father had accepted His sacrifice. But though hope faded, trust in His Father did not. By faith He was victorious.

Everyone who goes through to the kingdom will experience days of darkness and deep perplexity. It is easy to trust God when all is sweetness and light and His smile is upon us, but it is not easy when God apparently has forsaken us and we are struggling alone in the dark. Dark days are necessary, however, to prepare us for the still darker days that are ahead, even the time of Jacob's trouble, when every appearance will be against us and we will seemingly be left alone.

There are times when we feel discouraged and alone. The heavens are as brass above us, and no light comes through. We feel abandoned and forsaken. God seems to be far off. If He still loves us, why does He not come to our rescue? We are passing through the valley, and all is dark. We pray, but no one hears; we weep, but we weep alone.

Then, as we pray and agonize, we really see God as He is. The veil is drawn aside, and we behold Him who loved us and gave His only Son for us. At the center of the universe is not an impersonal God, not an absentee landlord, not a judge, but a loving Father, one who is touched with the feelings of our infirmities and whose great heart of love yearns over us. We catch a view of Gethsemane and Golgotha.

What a revelation this is! God Himself has suffered; He has passed through the deep waters; He has known loneliness and despair! He undersands, and He loves me.

Thank God, we need not feel alone any more. We

have a God in heaven who knows and cares; we have a friend at court who will take our part. Why, then, should we be discouraged, why downhearted? Why should we murmur or complain? God knows our temptations, our loneliness, our weaknesses; but He does not despise us. There is not a sorrow or disappointment we endure that He has not felt.

We need be dismayed no more, for we are children of a king. We have God, who knows and loves us. He bears us on the breastplate of His love; He goes with us all the way, even through the dark valley. Ever blessed be the God of our love!

It is not true, as some would have us believe, that the pathway to heaven is strewn with roses. There are roses, indeed, but there are also thorns, and many of the thorns are sharp, and they pierce deep. But if we walk with God, He will help us over the worst places; if we cling to Him, He will see us through. If darkness comes, we only need to clasp His hand a little tighter, and precious will be the seasons we will have with Him in the dark.

So let the perplexed and praying soul take courage. The way may not seem open and clear to us; but God is leading, and we can safely trust in Him. So, if the reader is one of those who fear the Lord and obey the voice of His servants, "let him trust in the name of the Lord, and stay upon his God."